Barnett Baff And The Everlasting Murder Case

To Eleanor,
Thank you for your
encouragement,
Bonnie

By Bonnie Quint Kaplan

Quint Publications
Rockport, MA

ISBN: 0615923852
ISBN-13: 978-0615923857

I was a child when my mother told me that her grandfather, Barnett Baff, had been murdered. He had been in the kosher poultry business and refused to go along with a price fixing scheme. His business rivals had sent a bomb to his home, but it did not go off. He had been offered police protection, but had refused it. His business rivals hired gangsters to kill him. One evening, on his way home from work, he had been ambushed and murdered.

It wasn't until my own children were almost grown that I discovered the truth. Barnett had been murdered, but the entire story was far more complex and protracted than I had been given to understand. It was a story of truth stranger than fiction that had never been fully assembled until I stumbled onto it.

To Dave, David, Beverly and Barnett

"I come from a long line of survivors."

- Martin Loonan
Early Member of American Mensa

Table of Contents

Kaleidoscope

Have you ever looked through a kaleidoscope, a child's toy of cardboard tubes, mirrors and colored fragments? When I was little, my parents had an antique version. It was much larger than my toy version, made of wood, metal, and colored glass. Its patterns were bigger and more intricate despite the finite nature of its particles. They evoked the rose windows of the gothic revival churches in my neighborhood, buildings whose purpose was, in childhood, a mystery to me.

My parent's kaleidoscope was also more fragile than a child's toy. It broke and disappeared from our home. I can't offer you a chance to look at those intricate and changing patterns. Instead I offer you an old kaleidoscope of people, places and events. The elements will recombine most intricately. There will be gangsters and businessmen, though it may be hard to tell the difference, immigrants, citizens, government, New York City, wholesale and retail, brownstones, gravestones and most definitely murder. I will show you the elements combined and, unlike the kaleidoscope, draw a narrative out of the fragments.

* * *

I was still a child when my mother told me that her grandfather, Barnett Baff, had been murdered. As a child, I did not find this unusual, because my mother did not present it as unusual. She just talked about it as a fact of life. As a child, I thought of my family and my life as normal. Besides, I lived in a post-Holocaust community of German Jewish Refugees. If I had told anyone that my great-grandfather was murdered, I would have been in good company.

However, my great-grandfather had met his end in America, in New York City, in the early twentieth century. He had been in the retail kosher poultry business. He had refused to go along with a price fixing scheme. His business rivals had sent a bomb to his home, but it did not go off. He had been offered police protection, but had refused it. His business rivals hired gangsters to kill him. One evening, on his way home from work, he had been ambushed and murdered.

Since my grandfather, Irving Baff, never talked about the murder case, my mother's knowledge of it came largely from her mother. Unfortunately, Grandma Hattie Baff (nee Hedvig Mayer) was not known for her reportorial precision*.

However, I lived with her version of Barnett's murder well into my 50's.

By this time, my mother was well into her 80's and sporadically cleaning out her house. She found the family documents that her father had given her when he was making his penultimate move to a nursing home. I took the documents, mostly relating to Irving, and made copies.

When my daughter, Nadine, and I were examining her copies, we noticed that Irving had been born in a hospital. We Googled the hospital and discovered that it was a maternity hospital that was only three or four years old when Irving was born. He had been part of the late nineteenth century trend away from home births.

The only document in the lot that was not about Irving was an official copy of Barnett's citizenship certificate. He had become a citizen in 1888. I hadn't realized that he had been in New York City for so much of the nineteenth century. He was the first of my ancestors to come to the United States. I decided to Google him too.

---

* In introducing my parents, Hattie managed to describe an American born, Russian Jewish, graphic designer of liberal leanings, as a Communist writer for a newspaper, who looked Italian.

Unbeknownst to me, my timing was perfect. Within the previous month, The New York Times had made its early twentieth century archives freely available.

I went on to find over one hundred articles on the murder, its prelude and aftermath. It turned out to be a classic experience of discovering the world through one's own eyes instead of through family tradition. It was true that Barnett had rejected price fixing and it was true that he had been murdered, but the two were only tangentially related. He had had police protection and I found out why the bomb, at his house, did not explode. Yes, gangsters had been hired to kill him, but not on his way home from work. Far from being overpowered in a sparsely populated setting, he was murdered in a crowded, public place. The aftermath was protracted as well. Though my mother hadn't known it, the case was still not closed when she was born half a dozen years after the murder.

I went on to share all the newspaper articles with Irving's descendents. My mother, wondered "who Barnett was before he became famous by not being." My friend, Howard Passel, told me about the City Directories and the Map Room at the New York Public Library. My son's social studies teacher, Bruce Baskind, recommended a little background reading. The Central Branch of the Brooklyn Public Library offered free access to Ancestor.com.

I realized that Barnett, like me, had moved to Brooklyn, albeit permanently. I visited his grave and stood in the spot where his shocked and grieving family had once stood. This was the turf to which my grandfather had returned for his mother, Fannie's burial, but not his own. In a separate expedition, I got within a short distance of the now indistinguishable spot of the murder. Barnett kept getting closer to me. Little by little, I gathered the shards of events and formed them into Barnett's story.

* * *

Barnett Baff

If only a hypothetical Time Magazine of 1914 had done a cover story on Barnett Baff, "The Poultry King". We'd know where he came from and when, how he got here, what his family life was, his legal and business entanglements, why and how he ended up dead on a New York City street, by the waterfront.

Absent finding a well researched narrative written almost a hundred years ago, one must research a cold trail. There are general books on the great migration of which Barnett's coming to America was a part and background odds and ends on the Internet. There are documents of his time, e.g. printed city directories and handwritten censuses. There are also the newspaper articles on the Poultry Trust prosecution and on the murder of Barnett.

What follows is what I've been able to piece together of Barnett's life, death, and post mortem events. While I quote freely from the New York Times, when I feel that I "couldn't have said it better," they report events as they were revealed. I had to sift out the facts, find the patterns and weave the story.

Of the thousands of impoverished, semi-skilled Russian and Eastern European Jews who came to America in the late nineteenth century, how did this one, Barnett Baff, come to incite his own bloody end? Of all the many murders committed, why would this one be difficult to carry out and shock the public? Why would it prove difficult to prosecute and end with a seeming lack of justice?

Arrival on the Shore of Time

The kaleidoscope turned, the DNA mixed and baby Barnett Baff arrived in about 1862,[1] in the Jewish Pale of Settlement, in Russia's Empire. His parents were Wolf Baff and Yetta Cohen, "his" Tsar was Alexander II. Based on the much later birth of his brother, Samuel, he may have been an eldest son. Barnett's future wife, Fannie (a.k.a. Frances) Berman (or Baermann), was born in 1861 or 1862.[2] She too was in the unfortunate position of being a Jewish subject of the Russian Tsar.

Half a world away, the United States was fighting its Civil War. Neither Abraham Lincoln nor any of his predecessors had been assassinated. However, gun technology was improving. The U.S. boasted a highly developed transportation system of canals and railroads. Food could be shipped long distances which meant an extensive system of middle men developed between farmers and housewives. This would set the stage for Barnett's future business.

Barnett and Fannie were married not later than the beginning of 1881, in Russia. We know this, because their first son, Harry, was born in December of 1881.[3] In order to have become a citizen in 1888, Barnett would have had to come to the U.S. no later than 1883. Harry and Fannie joined him in 1884.[4] Following a pattern that was to become common in immigration of the time, Barnett arrived, as a married man, then got established enough to send for his wife and young son.

Barnett's and Fannie's other surviving children were born much later. There were also various pregnancies that miscarried or children who did not survive.[5] Three children, besides Harry, lived to adulthood and even old age: William, born around 1892, Etta, born 1894, and Abraham, called Isadore and eventually Irving, was last, in 1897.

Leaving Europe

Based on his burial affiliation, Barnett was from Bialystock[6] in present day Poland. At the time that he left Bialystock, it was part of Russia, part of the Pale of Settlement, at the western border of Russia. It was an area to which Russia restricted its Jews. Jews were restricted from professions and education and variously persecuted. The freeing of the serfs, in 1861, further decreased the Jews' economic niche. Many Jews were dirt poor, semi-skilled labor. Bialystock would have helped prepare Barnett for city living. Work in its textile industry could have provided rudimentary tailoring skills. Barnett's youth helped make it possible to pull up stakes and probably stoked his sense of adventure. His need to support a family would have given economic impetus to his move.

The kaleidoscope of society was set in motion. New ideas were coming from Western Europe and the traditional, religious life, under the Rabbis' authority, was beginning to crumble. There was movement from the shtetl (little town), to the cities, to America. Around 1870, German steamship companies began to market their services to Eastern Europeans. One of the motivations was that people were a cost saving cargo that would load and unload themselves from a ship.

In 1881, about the time that Barnett was a married, young man, the old Tsar of the Russian Empire, Alexander II, was assassinated. The wheel turned: His more repressive and anti-semitic son, Alexander III, succeeded him. The upsurge in anti-semitism was felt in the form of pogroms, anti-Jewish riots. Barnett could read the handwriting on the wall. He needed to take his life into his own hands before he and his family were killed. He needed to seek his fortune while he was young and strong. He needed to join the Bialystokers who had already started their own congregation in America. If he never saw his parents again, there would be other children to comfort them in their old age. Based on his later actions, we know that he was a questioner of authority; he was a grasper of opportunity. He was going to America.

Barnett was far from unusual in leaving home. From 1870 until World War I, over one third of Eastern European Jews emigrated. This, like the flight from the Iberian Peninsula, caused by the Inquisition of 1492, and the exodus from Egypt, in Biblical times, was one of the great Jewish

Migrations and the largest. In the earlier part of the departure from Tzarist Russia, it was the less religious, less political and intellectual who pulled up stakes. They often did so over the objections of their parents who knew that they'd probably never see them again. One might succeed in America or not, but returning to the Russian Empire was unlikely. Once the pattern dissolved, it could not be restored.

In this increasingly well-worn play book, most of the Jews went to New York City. Around 1878, the Chevrah Anshei Chesed of Bialystock (Barnett's congregation) got its start on the Lower East Side of Manhattan Island. By 1893, there was a second Bialystoker congregation. The two congregations merged in 1905, in part to pool their resources and buy a former church building for more space. This former Methodist Church was built of locally quarried Manhattan Schist.

The congregation is still in that home, on Willett Street, between Grand and Broome Streets. Today, this section of Willett Street is known as Bialystoker Place. The synagogue has a carved ark of the covenant covered in gold filigree and a richly painted interior. It harks back to the painted wooden synagogues of Poland. However, when

Barnett arrived in the early 1880's, the setting for services was not so grand. It was a mere shtiebel, less than a synagogue. Barnett would have sat in one of the rows of chairs in a rented railroad flat. There would have been two rows at the back, for women, separated from the men by a curtain. Behind the women would have been the kitchen.

* * *

If Barnett followed the usual pattern, he would have left Bialystock traveling on foot, by coach or train, to somewhere near the border with Germany. Then, possibly with the paid help of a smuggler, he would have sneaked out of Russia into Germany. He would have proceeded north to depart from the port of Hamburg, Bremen, Antwerp or some other Northern European city.

Once Barnett had passed the medical inspection and didn't come to harm at the hands of those who cheated and exploited emigrants, he would have departed for New York City. For about $25, he would have sailed in steerage for as long as three weeks.

Steerage was the lowest deck of the ship to house people. As many as two thousand people would be crowded into rows of narrow bunk beds. There would be sections for single men, single women and families. As the voyage went on, the space became dirtier, smellier and less sanitary. The usual sustenance was herring, black bread and tea, staples of the poor Eastern European Jew. However, that was only when people weren't too seasick to eat. The crossing was a disorienting experience, but for Barnett there was no turning back. He had motive, means and wanted all the opportunities that he might find ahead.

Intriguingly, there is a ship's passenger list for the Waesland, out of Antwerp, Belgium that lists a 24 year old tailor, named Berl Baff, traveling in steerage and arriving in NYC, December 1881. Apart from timing, I haven't found anything definitive to connect Berl to the man who was called Barnet, Barnett, Bernard and Bernhard and whose business was B. Baff & Son. However, Berl could well have been Barnett's Hebrew name which was later anglicized.

Greenhorn in New York City

Barnett arrived in New York City at the Castle
Clinton Immigration Center established in 1855.
This location had morphed through time. Formerly
a fortification, it became the famous theater, Castle
Garden. In 1876, the theater was destroyed by fire
leaving only the old walls of the fort, but it was
swiftly rebuilt. (Earlier immigration had been
through the more chaotic docks on South Street.
Later immigration, after 1892, was funneled
through Ellis Island under the aegis of the U.S.
Government. Later immigrants, after 1886, were
also greeted by the Statue of Liberty.).

New York State, rather than the Federal
Government, oversaw Castle Clinton. It did a
shabby job with those immigrants who had to stay
overnight, letting them sleep on benches or floors,
and cheating them all when it could. They were
subjected to overpriced railroad tickets and
restricted choices of railroads and routes. The
baggage charges were excessive, the currency
exchange rates poor. Outsiders might get into the
immigration compound peddling fake savings
accounts and patronage employees of New York
State could be personally abusive. If Barnett

arrived in 1881, he also would have had to pay a dollar to the State for inspecting him. This charge wasn't declared unconstitutional, by the Supreme Court, until October 1882.

Barnett arrived approximately 20 years after the Civil War draft riots. The gangs that fomented those riots, the corrupt politicians who countenanced them and the ineffectual police force that could not quell them were still the norm. Lincoln had been assassinated and President Garfield too. Chester A. Arthur, a New Yorker, was President. In 1884, another New Yorker, Grover Cleveland, was elected president.

In 1881, New York City, which was only Manhattan Island, was gas lit. There were no steel framed skyscrapers. The whole country had fewer than 40 states. The Mormons were still practicing polygamy and the U.S. Army was still fighting to conquer its native population. There was no economic safety net, little law and order and streets full of horse manure, but also opportunity. The United States was recovering from the Panic (Recession) of 1873. New York City was connected to the rest of the country by canal, railroad and telegraph and to Europe by ship and transatlantic cable. It was well on it's way to being the epicenter of gilded age business success and wealth. Even had Barnett been born in New York City, he would have needed an appetite for change to deal with its constant evolution.

If we want to picture Barnett arriving as Berl, in December 1881, we can picture him leaving Castle Clinton with a group of other immigrants. They might have been accompanied by a representative of the Hebrew Emigrant Aid Society, started earlier that year. Despite the nippy weather and early sunset, the chance to walk on solid ground and see the City would have been a draw.

As the group started up Broadway, they would have passed the small, fenced in, Bowling Green Park that remained from the days of the Dutch settlers, the first Europeans in New York City. Their New Amsterdam had been a commercial colony and their Bowling Green was now surrounded by shipping offices and other businesses that formed the commercial hub of the City. The group walking along probably would not have known it, but they were passing near the first kosher butcher shop in New Amsterdam. It was licensed in 1661 to Asser Levy, like Barnett, a wandering Jew with Polish origins. The United States had recently celebrated its centennial, but

New York and its Jewish Community had roots more than 200 years old.

Barnett would have seen telephone and telegraph lines strung overhead as he passed between stone buildings, some as tall as 10 stories. The businesses would have sported hand painted signs in a language and alphabet that would have been entirely foreign to a Yiddish speaking Jew. Horse drawn vehicles would have filled the cobble stoned gutters. The sidewalks would have been paved with huge blocks of granite and bluestone or cast iron and glass sky lights for the basements below the street. At intervals, Barnett might have noticed that the sidewalk was punctuated with the cast iron covers of coal chutes.

As the new arrivals walked up Broadway, they would have passed a branch of Delmonico's Restaurant at Pine Street. Near City Hall, they would have angled northeast along Newspaper Row, officially labeled Park Row in the language that they were yet to master. As they continued north and east, they would have viewed the stone towers of the Brooklyn Bridge still under construction. Skirting Chinatown, they passed within a stone's throw of First Shearith Israel Graveyard, New York's first Jewish Cemetery dating back to 1683.

Continuing up East Broadway would have brought them to the immigrant slum of the Lower East Side.

Barnett, and then his family, was part of the wave of immigrants that turned the Lower East Side into a Jewish neighborhood. Barnett arrived right after the advent of the later despised Dumbbell Tenement. The Dumbbells had dismal airshafts, but their predecessors didn't even have those limited sources of light and air. The new comers lived in housing that was dark, poorly ventilated and overcrowded. At that, they could only afford it, because people shared apartments and often used them as places of business too. The typical diet was heavy on herring, bread, tea, potatoes, horseradish, carrots, cabbage, beets, fruit and cheap, fatty cuts of meat.

Residents usually didn't have bathtubs, but went to bathhouses. Bathing was not a daily ritual for most of contemporary society. A bed might be no more than a mattress on the floor. The high population density was a great breeding ground for diphtheria, influenza, typhoid, pneumonia and tuberculosis. However, through most of human history, both rich and poor have needed good immune systems to survive.

The Lower East Side was a point of entry and Barnett, Fannie and Harry might not have been living so badly compared to living in Bialystock. Besides, as Jews in Bialystock, they could never be more than second class citizens. This was America; this was different.

Barnett had come to the land of the Horatio Alger story. These novels, written by Horatio Alger, Jr. for a young audience, were success stories. Their poor, but honest and hard working heroes were able to triumph in the cities of America by their determination, effort and ability. Alger provided a moral tone which suggested that if a man didn't shirk, if he were morally and legally correct, he would be protected from failure. Alger's stories of self-made men had already been popular for more than a decade when Barnett, hardworking, law abiding and determined, became a part of urban America.

In New York City, Barnett might have worked as a street peddler or found employment as a garment worker, both occupations from a Horatio Alger Story. He would have lived as frugally as possible to send money back home and to buy steamship tickets for Fannie and Harry to join him in New York. If Barnett arrived in December of

1881, it was more than two years before his family was reunited at Castle Clinton.

Between 1881 and the arrival of Fannie and Harry, in 1884, events were moving in New York City and the U.S.A. With impetus from the inventions of Thomas Edison and others, New York City's streetlights were changing from natural gas to electric power. The Brooklyn Bridge had been opened to great fanfare. The Civil Service was established putting the Federal Government on a professional footing. Herman Hollerith was inventing the punch card technology that eventually gave IBM its start. Mark Twain was writing *Huckleberry Finn.* In 1882 Standard Oil pioneered the monopolistic business model of combining several businesses into a trust to fix prices and squelch competition.

Grover Cleveland was elected President, the first Democratic President since the Civil War and the second New Yorker in a row to be President. Like Barnett, both Chester A. Arthur and Grover Cleveland had been born elsewhere, but settled in New York State. This was also true of many business leaders who came to New York City for access to capital markets and other business support networks. By 1883, they were displaying their wealth in mansions along Fifth Avenue. By the end of the century, Thorstein Veblen labeled their behavior: Conspicuous consumption.

Meanwhile, at the other end of the economic spectrum, more semi-skilled, Jewish refugees from Eastern Europe were arriving. They usually claimed to be "tailors" and went to work in sweatshops. If they accumulated a little capital from their measly wages, they started their own sweatshops, often in their own small apartments. This appears to be what Barnett did since he is listed in the city directory of 1887-1888 as a tailor, living and working at 130 Forsyth Street, on the Lower East Side. Perhaps living and working in the same place was one of the factors that enabled the Baff family to survive the dangerous 54 hour blizzard of March 1888. Though, power lines and gas lines were down, they could continue working, by candlelight, in their own home while others tried to brave snowdrifts up to 30 feet high to get to and from work. The electric light had been invented, but not the snow day or the sick day.

While Barnett was a tailor, Fannie and Harry may have worked alongside him using their dining table as a work table. They probably slept in a bedroom barely wide enough for their bed and got water from a communal faucet in the hallway.

It is through his Lower East Side congregational affiliation that Barnett was buried in Brooklyn's Washington Cemetery. However, it was in the nature of the American experience for immigrants to become less religiously observant. That might not have bothered Barnett very much, because if he had been extreme in his religious practice in Europe, he probably would not have emigrated as early as he did. He would have been loathe to give up the patterns of observance. Nothing I know indicates religious transition, in America, for Barnett, but he abandoned the traditional beard and payis (side curls) of an old country Orthodox Jew.

However, in times of trouble, one might bring an old folk custom into play. When his last born son was a sickly child, Barnett stopped calling him Abraham and called him Isadore. Isadore (later Irving) did not known his real name until he was drafted into the army, during World War I, and saw his birth certificate for the first time. The intent had not been to mislead Isadore, but to mislead the Malakh ha-Mavet (Angel of Death). In Jewish folklore, this messenger of God could be tricked into thinking that the person for whom he had been sent was nowhere to be found. He could look for Abraham and be fooled by finding Isadore. It couldn't have hurt since Irving did live into his upper 80's.

Irving did not keep kosher, worked on Saturday and only went to synagogue on the high holy days and for weddings and bar mitzvahs. However, in a nod to his heritage, Irving went to Rosh Hashanah and Yom Kippur services at an Orthodox Congregation of Eastern European Jews rather than the Reform Temple attended by his wife, Hattie, and her German immigrant family. It wasn't until Abraham "Abe" Beame became prominent in New York City politics, around 1970, that Irving ever referred to himself as Abe and then rarely.

Moving Uptown with Meat and Poultry

As we know, Barnett did not remain a tailor or garment manufacturer though it is the occupation listed on his citizenship papers. After he became a citizen in 1888,* he next appears, in the city directory of 1891-1892, as a grocer at 31 Henry Street, another Lower East Side location. He isn't listed again until 1897-1898 by which time he has a meat business at 231 West 27th Street, Chelsea.[7]

It's not surprising that Barnett ended up in the meat business. The requirements for kosher meat meant that Jews needed to be active in the kosher meat business. As more and more Jews arrived in New York City, the demand for kosher meat increased. Jews hired other Jews to work in the meat business and the Jewish community increased its expertise in both kosher and non-kosher meat and poultry. It is estimated that by 1900, 80% of New York City's wholesale meat business and 50% of retail were owned by Jews.[8]

---

* Barnett became a citizen on October 19, 1888 in time to vote in the Presidential Election. The contest was between Grover Cleveland running for a second consecutive term and Benjamin Harrison who won.

Barnett had once again gone along with the pattern as the kaleidoscope turned.

While Barnett was growing his business, New York City was growing too. In 1898 it incorporated its twin city, Brooklyn, as well as Queens, The Bronx and Staten Island. That made it the world's second largest city with a population of three and a half million. Only London, England was more populous. And like London's parent country, New York's was becoming an imperial power. In 1898, the United States (45 States) had won the Spanish American War and been ceded the Philippines, Guam and Puerto Rico. That same year it annexed the Hawaiian islands. In 1903, it maneuvered Columbia into giving up Panama.

By the time Isadore/Irving was born, in 1897, Barnett and his family were living on West 27th Street. Barnett also had a meat business there. This was not the modern day Chelsea of art galleries and gentrification. It was part of the Tenderloin.* New York City's entertainment and red-light district.

---

* Though Tenderloin has become a generic term for red-light district, the term originated in New York City.

As of the 1900 census, 231 West 27th Street was still the location of Barnett's home and business. He had two boarders there, both butchers. It was customary to board the workers in a butcher shop as part of their meager compensation. This was different from taking in boarders on the Lower East Side which was done to help defray the rent on a tenement apartment.

In the 1901-1902 City Directory, the Baff family and business were still in Chelsea[9]. It was the start of a decade in which over a million Jews would come to America. Most would come to New York City and some would swell the ranks of Barnett's customers.

In 1890, the Sherman Anti-Trust act had been passed, but not enforced by the U.S. Supreme Court. New York State had passed the Donnelly Act, in 1899, assessing treble damages against those whose acts were harmful to competition. However, in business, trusts were still going strong and the consumer be damned. In the first decade of the new century, Barnett would find himself contending with the trust model.

The United States circa 1900 was an unfettered business climate in which Barnett and everyone around him functioned. Organized labor and government regulations were minimal. Income tax was non-existent. The Port of New York was celebrated in the Beaux-Arts Custom House built between 1902 and 1907. The City's capitalism and industry towered over the man in the street in such structures as the Metropolitan Life Insurance Company Tower and the Woolworth Building.

Barnett also lived in times of social idealism that took the form of organizing labor, support for Russia's failed 1905 revolution and social reforms through establishing settlement houses and sporadic anti-Tammany political reform. There were also consumer riots over the price of kosher meat, possibly an influence on Barnett's eventual decision to undersell other retailers. From the website of the *International Herald Tribune,* we learn what happened on the Lower East Side, in May 1902:

> Meat riots on a big scale have occurred here. Last Sunday [May 11] 400 kosher butchers on the East side instituted [and then abandoned] a boycott of the packers because of the high price of meat. But the women of the Ghetto, over five hundred of them, indignant over what they considered a cowardly capitulation to the packers, formed themselves into committees and began operations. They raided butcher's shops, tore the meat to pieces, flung some into ash

barrels, and what they could not carry they sprinkled with kerosene.

Barnett continued to prosper in the meat business and to roll northward on Manhattan Island. His partners in some of his locations were his oldest son, Harry, and his brother, Samuel[10]. Samuel Baff was Barnett's much younger brother. According to Samuel's World War I draft record, he was born on March 21, 1882. As such, he was a contemporary of Barnett's son, Harry. This was a time when women had children as long as they were fertile and hoped that some survived. Barnett's wife, Fannie, followed this model; of nine births, she had four surviving children.

Barnett probably paid Samuel's passage from Bialystock, to a European Port, to New York Harbor. In any event, Samuel followed Barnett to New York City in 1900 and worked with him. He died without issue in 1948 and was buried in the Barnett Baff family plot at Washington Cemetery.

Barnett's family continued to distance themselves from the Lower East Side. From Chelsea, they went North to East Harlem* and, by

---

* It is interesting to note that when he was living in East Harlem and Barnett was still alive, Isadore/Irving was already

1913, to Harlem proper. They had lived in a tenement and in an apartment over their business, but finally they moved into a handsome brownstone of their own, 76 West 120th Street. Of all the homes associated with Barnett, this seems to be the only one standing today. Built in 1899, today it is part of the Mount Morris Historic District, near Mount Morris Park, a.k.a. Marcus Garvey Park. (See photo which follows.).

At the time that Barnett lived in his Harlem brownstone, near Lenox Avenue, this was an upscale Jewish neighborhood. Here successful Russian and Eastern European Jews mixed with earlier arriving German Jews. Further East, around Madison and Fifth Avenues, where Barnett's family had lived in an apartment, was a middle class Jewish neighborhood. Still further

---

working in the family business. He would occasionally use his earnings to eat out, with his friends, at Finestone's delicatessen at 1655 Madison Avenue. When they got rowdy, as teenagers will, the restaurant's proprietor, George Finestone, would have to ask them to leave. George, and his wife, Anna, were also part of the great migration of Russian and Eastern European Jews to the U.S. at the turn of the Century. (George arrived in the U.S. by 1909 when he married Anna, in Brooklyn.) Ultimately, George and Anna's son, Bernard, married Irving's daughter, Beverly. Irving and George were reunited, on friendly terms, at the wedding.

East were Jewish slums absorbing the overflow of poor immigrants from the Lower East Side.[11]

76 West 120th Street
New York, New York

West Washington Market

The City Directory of 1910-1911 lists Barnett's wholesale poultry business at 60 Thompson Avenue, West Washington Market. However, it had been there since at least 1906. Completed in 1889, West Washington Market was a meat market to complement the nearby Gansevoort Farmers' Market opened ten years earlier. It was west of today's increasingly fashionable Meat Packing District. (See map which follows.) It was a City owned market. Today, its site, between West Street and the river, is used by the City's Department of Sanitation to park garbage trucks.

Like much of the City's industry, the West Washington and Gansevoort Markets took advantage of the convenient transportation options that came with the City's waterfront. The Pennsylvania Railroad and many other lines ran freight trains to the docks of New Jersey and then ran them onto barges with rails on their decks. Tug boats powered the barges across the mile wide Hudson River, also known as the North River, to the docks of Manhattan.

Except for various connections to the Bronx, across the Harlem River, in 1906 Manhattan had two bridges across the East River and only Ferries to cross the Hudson River. The only direct connection, for horse drawn or motorized truck traffic, from the New Jersey rail yards to the Westside of Manhattan was by fording the Hudson River on a ferry. Today's large number of motorized vehicles, tunnels and bridges make it hard to picture the crowded River traffic of 1906.

The meat and poultry industries received shipments from the Midwest and other parts of the United States at the rail yards in Weehawken and Hoboken.[12] Tough men, known as chicken pullers, unloaded crates of live chickens and sorted them into cages for consignment to wholesalers. Some of the chicken pullers worked for brothers Harry, Jacob and Joseph Cohen who held contracts for unloading poultry.

Taking a break from their heavy, smelly work, the chicken pullers hung out in bars. From time to time they had to change hang outs, because bars blew up. While the owners made excuses that they were bombed by enemies or their customers were making fireworks, it is probable that the saloons doubled as bomb factories. The bars were also the "offices" of gangsters. They stored their guns there and left messages and even money, for each other, with the bartender. The saloon was a place to plan crimes too.[13]

By 1906, the Manhattan Refrigerating Company had cemented West Washington Market's place as the center of the City's meat trade. This leading edge company laid pipe under the streets of the market. It provided cold water chilling to the market stalls greatly extending the shelf life of the meat. It modernized the technology of the meat business even as Barnett would modernize the economics of the kosher meat business. The wheels of change were in motion.

In 1906, subway technology was also in place, though just barely. The subterranean transit system was only two years old. The IRT subway connected Manhattan and the Bronx, but it would be another two years before it extended to Brooklyn. However, getting around the City was also possible by elevated trains.

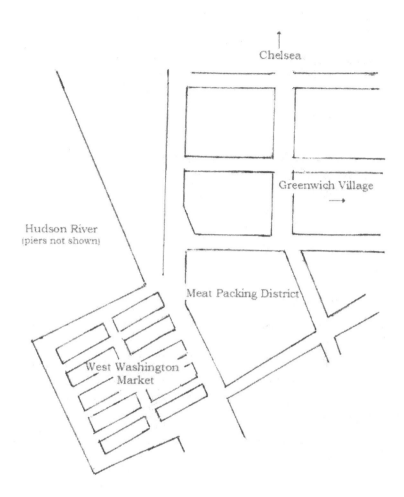

Chelsea

Greenwich Village

Hudson River
(piers not shown)

Meat Packing District

West Washington
Market

West Washington Market
and
Vacinity

The Poultry Trust

West Washington Market had disadvantages too. In summer it baked in the reflection off the Hudson River. In winter it was unprotected from the wind. The local fauna, homo sapiens sapiens, were dangerous too.

A pattern of doing business came into focus, in 1906, when a large group of live poultry merchants joined together as the New York Live Poultry Commission Merchants Protective Association. This group, in West Washington Market and other areas of New York City, operated as a price fixing Poultry Trust and tried to keep stands, in the Market, out of the hands of independent dealers.

Barnett was not a big chicken dealer at this time, but he was "pronounced in his views of the right and wrong ways of doing business."[14] If the Poultry Trust wanted to control prices, Barnett would receive his own independent shipments of chickens. Then the Western shippers would not be dependent on the Trust for all their New York City business.

The Trust responded with harrasment. They complained anonymously to the City Health

Department that the independent dealers were selling live poultry. Then, through misinformation or corruption, the Health Department threatened to revoke the permits of the independents despite the fact that what they were doing was legal. It was also brought out, in a hearing before the Committee on Laws and Legislation of the City Alderman,[15] that the slaughterhouses and cart drivers were in the pocket of the Trust and not working with the independents. The Sherman Anti-Trust Act and the New York State Donnelly Act existed, as examples of changing sentiment, but hadn't yet been put into practice. In fact, the poultry trust would eventually be indicted under a 40 year old New York State anti-conspiracy law.

Barnett saw the pattern and would not be stopped by the Trust. The independents took their case to the Aldermen, (predecessors to the New York City Council), and also to the Manhattan District Attorney, William Travers Jerome, (a double first cousin of Winston Churchill's mother*). Though considered by many to be a reformer, Mr. Jerome denied that the Poultry Trust was violating

---

* William Travers Jerome's and Jennie Jerome Churchill's fathers were brothers. Their mother's were sisters.

New York State's anti-trust laws. However his Assistant D.A., Charles C. Nott, Jr.*, did not agree. Later Mr. Nott was to testify,

> "A delegation composed of independent dealers in live poultry called on me during the latter part of Mr. Jerome's administration and informed me that the so-called trust was forcing them out of business. After hearing their complaint I decided that the association was violating the anti-trust law, and told them that I was ready to prosecute. I informed them that they should furnish further data, but gave them to understand that they could not use the District Attorney's office to force the association to take them in as members. The delegation grinned and left."[16]

Barnett Baff was one of those grinning independent poultry dealers. He had become familiar with the Poultry Trust, but broke away and could provide the inside knowledge that enabled the District Attorney's office to prosecute. He was not just surviving in the business climate of his time, but starting to reinvent the way business was done. He was turning the wheel, letting the pattern fall to pieces and letting the elements reorganize.

---

* Charles Nott also had a Churchill connection. His wife, Julia Jerome Hildt, was a second cousin of Winston Churchhill and a first cousin once removed of William Travers Jerome.

The varied reception of the independents' complaint on the part of Mr. Jerome and Mr. Nott was typical of the times. Mr. Jerome, in this, was an official looking the other way and Mr. Nott demonstrated one of the spasms of reform with which lawlessness was sporadically met. There is some evidence that though Mr. Jerome was known as a reformer, he did not care about reforming big business[17].

By the time that poultry dealers of the trust were indicted, in March 1910, Mr. Jerome had further revealed his character by becoming their defense attorney. The case, against 19 of the trust members, came to trial, in June 1911, prosecuted by Assistant District Attorney William De Ford, the District Attorney's anti-Trust specialist. He and Mr. Jerome not only each pursued his own side of the case, but were mutually antagonistic. Mr. De Ford, who came from Kansas, was accused, by Mr. Jerome, of representing the interests of the, supposedly monopolistic, Mid-Western packing-houses. Mr. Jerome contended that the Poultry Trust was merely a combination to resist the heavy hand of the packinghouses.

Mr. De Ford met this accusation with great sarcasm:

"The gentleman's suggestions have the subtlety and delicacy for which he is famous. The distinguished gentleman suggests that the District Attorney, acting perhaps as the agent for the great packing companies, is prosecuting this little monopoly here that the monopoly here may be brought to book for their exactions. The suggestion is quite worthy of the gentleman as I look back on the gentleman's career. The gentleman has expressed himself very feelingly about our solicitude for the great packing companies, and has asked why we have not prosecuted that giant trust. I would like to ask the gentleman what he was doing in the office of the District Attorney for eight years when those trusts were operating here?

"I would like to ask the gentleman what he was doing in the office of the District Attorney when this combination was being organized under his very nose? You are a splendid specimen of a professional gentleman to dare walk into this courtroom and question the integrity of this administration in its relations to one of the big trusts that dominated the industry in this country. And I reject it, Sir, not only as a false suggestion, but I point it out as typical of the gentleman's candor and as typical of his professional integrity. Now, I think you can understand that, Sir, and you can answer it if you want to."

Mr. Jerome, who had been standing up all the time, took an exception to Mr. De Ford's remarks, and Judge Rosalsky cautioned the jury to disregard all that passed between the two men.[18]

The next day in court was no better. Mr. Jerome defended his record and accused Mr. De Ford of being a fanatic. Mr. De Ford then detailed Mr. Jerome's refusal as D.A. to prosecute various trusts. Mr. Jerome, far from defending his actions, then accused Mr. De Ford of shirking military service. Mr. De Ford later explained his honorable resignation from military service in a very plausible manner.

Mr. Jerome may have been particularly optimistic about the tactic of getting under Mr. De Ford's skin. About a year before the trial, Mr. De Ford had had a nervous breakdown after the death of his wife and child. Shortly after the trial concluded, Mr. De Ford had a second breakdown .[19]

Despite the friction of the attorneys, the case eventually concluded with the jury finding thirteen of the defendants guilty, four not guilty. (Charges had been dropped against an ill defendant and a female defendant.). In his statement, thanking the jury, Judge Rosalsky also said,

> "There was no doubt in my mind but that these defendants with criminal intent committed acts injurious to trade, that they throttled competition. They drove men who

were entitled to be legitimately in business out of it ... They violated a law upon the statute books and they must pay the penalty by serving a prison sentence.

"The law must be enforced. This is the first conviction within my recollection under the law. If these defendants had pleaded guilty and submitted themselves to the court their sentence would have been different. Instead they put the people to the expense of a trial and challenged the State of New York to prove their guilt ... I shall commit the defendants to the Tombs*."[20]

Mr. Jerome proceeded to criticize Judge Rosalsky's reference to the cost of the trial. This provoked an angry response from Judge Rosalsky as well as criticism of Mr. Jerome's conduct when he was a judge. Not content to leave it at that, Mr. Jerome opined on Judge Rosalsky's decision to hold the prisoners, pending sentencing: "This is not only an act of injustice, but an act of oppression." It's not surprising that Judge Rosalsky then refused to free the prisoners on bail.

---

* By this time, the original Tombs Prison was gone. The original New York City House of Detention had been modeled on an Egyptian Mausoleum when it was built in 1838. Though it had been replaced by a Romanesque Revival building, its original nickname of "The Tombs" stuck.

The guilty defendants were convicted of conspiracy under Section 580 of the New York State Penal Law. Though the law was some 40 years old, this was the first time that the punishment for violating it included prison.   Judge Rosalsky, known for his stiff sentencing of criminals,[21] gave each of the monopolists a three month jail sentence and a $500 fine. A Republican[*] reformer and a Jew born on the Lower East Side, the Judge summed up the case with great passion:

> "A conspiracy to monopolize and control a food product ... is a mean and insidious crime stealthily committed and usually, if not always, by men who masquerade in the garb of good repute, but in whose breasts the quality of common morality has been stifled by the most despicable form of greed. It is the kind of crime upon which merchants wax fat at the expense of the poor and helpless consumers. The motives which induced these defendants to disregard public interest was selfish aggrandizement regardless of law."[22]

---

[*] In New York City, the Republicans were generally the party of reform, because the New York City Democrats were dominated by the leaders of Tammany Hall who believed in "honest graft". Reform Democrats did not start their rise to power until the 1960's. In 1978, Edward I. Koch became the City's first Reform Democratic mayor.

On August 25th, Mr. Jerome and Mr. De Ford were back in court. Mr. Jerome was asking to appeal the case based on technicalities. Mr. De Ford was trying to postpone the appeal, but the presiding Judge Bischoff was unsympathetic to a postponement.

Barnett must have been grinning again when the United States Packing Company sued the Poultry Trust members for triple damages of $225,000. The suit alleged price fixing that prevented the selling of live poultry, at a fair price, based on a free market. It was thought to be the first suit under the Sherman Anti-trust law seeking damages for restraining the sale of food products or, to quote Judge Rosalsky, "a necessary of life".[23] Suit was brought in November.

Finally, on February 6, 1914, the 13 dealers convicted in the Poultry Trust case lost their appeal. They each had to pay a $500 fine and serve three months in the penitentiary. Manhattan District Attorney, and later Governor of New York State, Charles S. Whitman was quite pleased with the outcome. He said, "it was the first conviction in the United States in which a jail sentence had been imposed on defendants [who were] found guilty of restraint of trade, [on which] an appeal [was] taken, and in which the judgment had been affirmed upon appeal."[24]

However, after being imprisoned briefly, the convicted men were released on bail pending one final appeal which was still in progress at the time of Barnett's death. At last, in May 1915, the outcome that had pleased Judge Rosalsky, Charles Whitman and Barnett Baff was unanimously affirmed by the New York State Court of Appeals. The fines had to be paid and the sentences served. The court system and its protections were working as designed. Though he didn't live to see the final affirmation, Barnett and his retail customers were benefiting from the rule of law.

Charles S. Whitman

This was not the only case whose outcome pleased District Attorney Whitman. In 1912 he won the conviction of Charles Becker for the murder of gambling club owner Herman Rosenthal. This case has been compared to the Barnett Baff case, because it also involved a public shooting. Another parallel: the Rosenthal murder was the second, in New York City, in which a getaway car was used. The Baff murder was the City's third use of a getaway car. Despite the technological similarities, the Rosenthal shooting did not involve a law abiding businessman. Rosenthal was a gangster.

Public gun violence affected the nation at levels high and low. In 1901, President William McKinley was shot, at a public event, by an anarchist. He died of his wounds a week later. Theodore Roosevelt succeeded to the Presidency. He too drew gunfire though not fatally and not until 1912.

Along with the public shooting of a prominent figure, there was the getaway car similarity between the Rosenthal and Baff cases. While it had to start somewhere, it's not surprising that the car was appropriated as a vehicle of escape. Once Henry

Ford started producing the widely affordable Model T, in 1908, the use of cars spread throughout the population.

What enhanced public interest in the Rosenthal case was that the accused mastermind, Charles Becker, was a corrupt cop. Then, as now, the rooting out of "bad" cops was politically popular. (It was one of the causes that helped William Travers Jerome become known as a prominent reformer.).

The case against Becker was thrown out on appeal and re-tried in 1914. It was the City's first re-conviction. It eventually sent Becker to the electric chair and crusading D.A. Whitman to the New York State Governor's Mansion. In fact, when Becker made his final appeal for executive clemency, Governor Whitman refused to recuse himself despite his history as prosecutor. As Governor, Whitman would play a role in the Baff Case and again fail to produce a clear sense of justice.

Independent

In 1908, Barnett's employees presented Barnett and Fannie with a silver kiddush cup[*] for their Silver Wedding Anniversary. One has to suspect this of being an Americanizing gesture since it comes later than their actual 25th anniversary. The cup has a Biblical quote, in Hebrew, "[May God] Grant thee according to thine own heart, /And fulfil all thy counsel." While this sounds like a basic wish of good fortune, it is from the 20th Psalm which goes on to employ militaristic imagery:

> We will shout for joy in thy victory,
> And in the name of our God we will set up our standards;
> The Lord fulfil all thy petitions.
>
> Now know I that the Lord saveth His annointed;
> He will answer him from His holy heaven
> With the mighty acts of His saving right hand.
> Some trust in chariots, and some in horses;
> But we will make mention of the name of the Lord our God.
> They are bowed down and fallen;
> But we are risen, and stand upright.

---

[*] A kiddush cup is filled with wine or grape juice, a blessing is recited and the cup is drained.

By 1908, Barnett was already embroiled in the business battles that would eventually consume him. This brings us to the ruthless, but legal business practices with which Barnett enraged his retail competitors, but not his customers. These occupied the last few years before his murder, on November 24, 1914, and contributed to his wealth of over $70,000 in World War I era dollars, over $1,600,000 today.

Barnett was an independent and ambitious poultry dealer. Through his business knowledge and brains, he created his own financially successful modus operandi and his own alliances. However his methods led to conflict with many factions of his industry. As the kaleidoscope turned, not everyone could roll on and keep up.

Here in the words of Barnett's friend, Herbert A. Emerson, Vice President and General Manager of the Live Poultry Auction Company, is what happened:

> "Before 1910 the poultry business in this city was controlled by a score or more of poultry receivers who have been called the trust. They were not a close organization, but they received all shipments of poultry from the West and had a monopoly on its distribution. By agreement they fixed the price of poultry

once a week and sold their stock to the retail buyers, whom we call the kosher killers. They are the men who take the live poultry from the markets, kill it according to their Jewish ritual, and then sell it to consumers direct or to small dealers."

"In the trust-controlled market these kosher killers played a safe game. They all bought poultry at a fixed price and sold it at a reasonable profit. No matter how high the price was, their profits were assured ... And the trust receivers protected them. None of the monopolists entered into competition with them or tried to undersell them in the retail trade."

"But Barnet Baff broke away from the poultry trust in 1910 and appeared in the field as the first independent receiver. He turned to the courts ... he completely smashed the trust. At about the same time A.T. Pearson was sent to New York from Chicago as the representative of the National Car Lot Poultry Shippers Association, an organization of Western poultry shippers who thought they had not been getting a square deal in New York."

"Pearson's job was to receive the shipments of the association and sell its poultry at the highest price obtainable. His first fight was with the poultry thieves in the New Jersey freight yards, and also he wanted an open market in which he might sell his poultry at the highest price. He therefore joined hands with Baff in fighting the poultry thieves and in breaking up the trust."

"Then the Live Poultry Auction Company came into the field. Realizing the demand for an open market where prices might be fixed daily by competitive bidding ... I was made the ... manager. I had been a Western shipper, and, in fact, shipped Baff the first carload of poultry received after he broke with the trust."

"We had then two big independent dealers and an open market ... The poultry industry was modernized. The auction company resembles a board of trade or stock exchange ..."

"But where were the kosher killers! Suddenly, they were thrown into a condition of chaos. They no longer were able to buy their poultry at a fixed price and sell it at a small profit, but had to go into an open market ... and take their chances in the trade. Many of them are immigrant Russian Jews, who have no idea of modern business methods and are not capable of contending in an open market with men of the brains and backing of Baff and Pearson. Even if Baff had remained a receiver and wholesaler the kosher killers would ... not know where to turn or what to do."

"But Baff was in the business to make money and he felt justified in making it in any honest way, so he used his brains and power to his own advantage and, in consequence to the disadvantage of the kosher killers. If he received a large shipment of poultry from the West naturally he wanted to get as high a price for it as possible, so he would go into the auction and, to use a stock exchange phrase, he would 'bull' the market. He would bid up prices and then sell his own stock independently or through the auction at the prevailing prices. Pearson naturally also insisted on obtaining the market prices for his stock."

"The kosher killers at first refused to buy from Baff or to accept the market prices so Baff got into the retail field. He opened several retail markets of his own and backed several butchers who bought exclusively from him. With his facilities for thus disposing of his stock he was able to 'bull' the market prices here above the prices at which he obtained his poultry from the West, and then undersell the kosher killers in the retail field. As he was about the largest independent receiver in the city, and the association of shippers represented by Pearson sent one-third of the poultry received in New York, the two, by simply going out into the open market were able to command a good deal of power."[25]

By "kosher killers", Emerson was really referring to Barnett's kosher, retail competition. They would envy Barnett's colorful and bright business design.

When H. A. Emerson described the confusion of the Russian Jewish immigrant retailers, did he realize that Barnett Baff was also a Russian Jewish immigrant? Whether he did or not, Barnett had pulled away from the pack to a different position from others of a similar background. He had been in the United States longer than many immigrants of his group. He had, in many ways, recovered from three shocks: being physically uprooted, leaving a traditional religious/cultural community and working his way up the economic ladder.[26]

Barnett came to the U.S. from a traditional community in which each member of the shul (temple) had his assigned status in the community. He left that place and those social rules behind and started with nothing, even his family was temporarily left behind. Then he had the chutzpah (nerve) to turn his displacement into a blank slate on which he created himself: Barnett Baff, independent poultry dealer. He had come to New York City as a poor tailor. Now, besides his businesses and those to which he loaned money, he had begun to invest in Real Estate, a classic Jewish immigrant path to wealth.[27] While others sought to chant a familiar ritual, Barnett was improvising wildly and shaking the kaleidoscope.

Barnett was the champion of the poultry shippers in Chicago, St. Louis and Southern cities and the friend of their New York Representatives.[28] The shippers were to send their own private detectives to West Washington Market after

Barnett's death and offer a reward for the arrest and conviction of his murderer.

Barnett had some retail allies too who undersold butchers who did business with other wholesalers. His friend, Alexander Perlman, was a retailer in the East New York Market (in Brooklyn). However, Perlman stopped buying from Barnett after being assaulted four times.

Besides his perfectly legal price manipulations, Barnett's attorney, Nathan H. Stone, was representing him in about 25 business-related lawsuits at the time of his death. Barnett had famously used the Manhattan District Attorney to prosecute the Poultry Trust and he worked with the New Jersey authorities to prosecute chicken thieves in the Jersey rail yards. Though organizing labor was often a Russian Jewish cause, Barnett used non-union labor. At one point this lead to his workers being attacked by union men.

Within the kosher meat business of the Russian Jewish community, Barnett pinned his success on his own wits and on the law. He controlled 10% of live poultry shipments coming into New York and did $300,000 a year in business. (That's almost seven million in today's dollars.).

Barnett was too big for his business rivals in the Live Poultry Dealers Protective Association to buy him out. Unlike the Poultry Trust, he wasn't breaking the law. In 1913, attempted mediation between Barnett and his poultry industry rivals, by Reform Rabbi Judah Magnes,* came to naught. Barnett was accused of unfair competition and ruthless methods. He accused his business rivals of dishonesty and combining against him. They had boycotted his wholesale business, but this had just lead him to become a retailer. They insisted that Barnett pay for chicken inspectors in the rail yards. When he refused, the inspectors accused him of sanding his chickens, i.e. feeding them sand to inflate their weights. Barnett was fined $40 over this.

---

* This was not the Rabbi of Barnett's congregation. Rabbi Magnes was working for a Jewish organization that was trying to establish a governmental structure for all the Jews of New York City. However, the attempt at government would have required bridging gaps among Reform, Conservative and Orthodox and among Sephardic Jews, German Jews and Russian/Eastern European Jews, older Americans and new ones. This attempt at government, like the attempt at mediating Barnett's disputes, was not successful. In fact, the mediation might have been seen as the more established, wealthier, Reform, German Jews having a paternalistic attitude toward the poorer, immigrant, Orthodox, Russian Jews.

By the Spring of 1914, Barnett was also at odds with Harry, Jacob, and Joseph Cohen, brothers who controlled the unloading of poulty in the New Jersey rail yards. They would make common cause with the retailers of the Live Poultry Dealers Protective Association in plotting against Barnett.

The Criminal Element

While Barnett was building his family business "in any honest way,"[29] there were, by contrast, the businesses started by Philip Musica and his family. His parents and perhaps Musica were immigrants from Naples, Italy. Just as the late nineteenth and early twentieth century were peak times of immigration by Eastern European Jews, they were also peak years for immigrants from Southern Italy. In New York City, these two groups of new arrivals lived and worked in close proximity especially on the Lower East Side and in Harlem. However, the Jews who had escaped from their old countries had in effect bought one-way tickets to America. The Italians were free to travel back and forth to Italy.

In 1909, Philip Musica, who had become a cheese importer, was convicted of bribing customs officials and served 5 months in jail. Next, with help from his father, who was a barber, he started the United States Hair Company. It appeared to traffic in human hair for wigs, but its main purpose was to get bank loans based on false financial records and possibly to sell worthless stock. In 1913, with authorities onto their scheme, the

Musicas attempted to escape to Honduras. They got as far as New Orleans before they were caught and brought back to New York City.

Philip took the blame for the entire $600,000 fraud and was incarcerated in the Tombs, New York City's jail. There he mingled with other gangsters including one Joseph Sorro. After confessing his financial scams to Manhattan District Attorney Charles Whitman, Philip became a star stool pigeon helping to convict other criminals. As a consequence, he was never "sent up the [Hudson] river" to Sing Sing prison in Ossining, New York. Musica was still in the Tombs when Barnett was murdered. At this point, the interests of Philip Musica and the Baff family had yet to conflict.

* * *

The years after the break up of the Poultry Trust were toward the end of the period covered by Herbert Asbury's *The Gangs of New York*. Barnett's murder does get mentioned toward the end of the book, on page 336, in a discussion of gangsters being used to intimidate business competitors.

In the early years of the Twentieth Century, criminal gangs and thugs hung around West Washington Market. They were there, because they were too uneducated or unsocialized to get better jobs in the legitimate economy and the economic safety nets of the New Deal lay in the future. Barnett's competitors had no trouble hiring them to target Barnett and his businesses in many illegal ways. He and his lawyer received threatening letters. His work horses were fed apples that were filled with hidden cyanide.[30] However, Barnett, in his adaptable way, dealt with the horse poisonings by changing over to motor vehicles. His livestock was poisoned or stolen; his crates were damaged. Two carloads of his poultry were blown up in the Weehawken rail yards. His retail market at 420 East 109th street was robbed though little was taken. Bombs were left at a store, at his Manhattan Residence and at his Arverne, Queens summer residence.

Barnett's oldest son and partner, Harry Baff, was beaten with an easily concealed blackjack. His bookkeeper was assaulted too; his business ally, A.T. Pearson, representative of the National Car Lot Poultry Shippers Association, was assaulted twice. When gang member David Clodney was arrested in December 1914 for the second assault on Pearson, he was taken to police headquarters.

While he was being conducted through the hall, [he] was accosted by Detective Dalton.

"Hello," said Dalton, "didn't I arrest you about two years ago for assaulting Baff's bookkeeper?"

"Yes." Growled [Clodney].[31]

Gangsters were semi-skilled labor doing business as usual.

Also arrested, in December 1914, were members of the Hudson Dusters gang. The police wondered if they had been involved in the murder of Barnett. The Hudson Dusters had come to the attention of the police by the actions of a different gang. Gopher gangsters had recently attacked the Hudson Dusters for the sin of cutting the price charged to poultry dealers for "jobs done" in West Washington Market.

Though the criminal life was rife with violence, it was also a way of earning money like any other job. This is particularly evident in the story of the bombing of Barnett's house at 3 South Summerfield Avenue,[32] Queens on July 11, 1913.[33] Frank Burke, Joe Sorro, and Tony Nino were going to split $300 for placing the bomb. They drove out to Arverne, a new real estate development, on the Rockaway Peninsula*.

---

* It is currently being redeveloped and marketed as "Arverne-by-the Sea".

At 10:30 p.m. they placed the bomb [on Barnett's porch] and sped back to the city ...[34] Barnett was about to sit in a hammock when he saw the bomb with its fuse burned, but not burning. He called the police who found that the bomb was filled with jagged pieces of scrap iron, steel slugs, and enough explosives to destroy Barnett's vacation cottage. [35]

> Later would-be bomber, Frank Burke was

> asked whether he knew that the explosion of the bomb would bring death to the inmates, [he] replied that he knew beforehand that the bomb would cause no harm, because, unknown to his accomplices, he had deliberately wet the fuse..."I was after the money and not the deed."[36]

However when Burke tried to collect his pay, he was asked to show proof, by way of a newspaper article, that the bomb had been set. He would later testify:

> "I then telephoned to the city editor of the New York World and asked him if he could give me any information with reference to the planting of a bomb at Baff's home in Long Island. He asked me to repeat my query, so I repeated. Then the city editor asked me to hold the wire until he got a better connection, because he could not hear very well. Naturally I didn't hold the wire."[37]

The next day, the World ran a story about the bomb. However, because the bomb had done little damage, Joseph Cohen said to Antonio Cardinale, "Hell you don't want me to pay $200 [sic] for that bum job."[38] The subsequent payment to the bombers was only $100. The man who hired the car and obtained the bomb got $35, $25 for the car and $10 for the bomb. The chauffeur of the car got a $5 tip. The three bombers split the rest: Burke, himself, receiving only $20.

The Plot Thickens

By the summer of 1914, Harry Baff was following his father protectively through the streets of West Washington Market.[39] On the world stage, this was the summer when Archduke Franz Ferdinand of Austria and his wife were shot by a Bosnian Serb separatist. Europe spent the summer headed to the battlefields of World War I.

As Barnett remained undeterred by the gangster-employing tactics of the Live Poultry Dealers Protective Association, his rivals became increasingly frantic. At one of their meetings, a woman who claimed that Barnett had driven her out of business stood on a chair shouting that "some one certainly would kill him."[40]

A twenty-two year old bartender, Carl Rettich, heard plotting in his father's Hoboken Saloon. Another man, a Martin Houlihan, of Jersey City claimed to hear plotting. Though Houlihan was probably just seeking attention, men might well have said of Barnett, as Houlihan claimed, "He can't be trusted. If we get him out of the way we can get his business."[41]

Though most of the members of the Live Poultry Dealers Protective Association did not know it, a plot, to murder Barnett, was taking shape. Starting in late May or early June, 1914, over a hundred poultrymen contributed to an anti-Baff fund thinking it might be used for a lawsuit. Amounts volunteered ranged from a few donations of hundreds of dollars to a larger number of $10 to $50 contributions.[42] What most poultrymen did not know was that a group of about a dozen were actually conspiring to murder Barnett. Of the four or five thousand dollars in their fund, they allocated $250 for the actual murder; the rest was for the defense of any of the conspirators who might need a lawyer.[43]

The desired murder had its challenges: It needed to be committed in a public market and the murderers should have as little connection as possible to the Live Poultry Dealers Protective Association. The latter problem was solved first. In 1913, Joseph Cohen, one of the inner circle of anti-Baff hot heads, met chicken dealer Antonio Cardinale.

At that time, Cardinale and his brother-in-law, Joe De Campo, had a retail store on West 110th Street, in Harlem's Little Italy. "He found himself unable to make the business go, and inasmuch as De Campo was eager to give it up, Cardinale was persuaded by Cohen to receive into partnership David Jacobs, Cohen's brother-in-law" and fellow plotter. "Prior to the beginning of the new [Italian-Jewish] partnership Cohen ... had already conceived the plan of putting a bomb under Baff's house at Arverne. "[44]

This was an era when Harlem was as much an immigrant neighborhood as the Lower East Side and the Little Italy (North of Canal Street). There were large numbers of both Jewish and Italian immigrants in East Harlem. (While the Jews moved on, there was an Italian presence as late as the 1970's.) In Barnett's day, it was a place where Italians and Jews might rub shoulders.

David Jacobs new partner, Cardinale, proved useful in hiring the Arverne bombers and purchasing the bomb at Ippolito Greco's saloon in East Harlem. This saloon, at 227 East 107th Street, was a place where criminals congregated and were hired for jobs. It became the employment agency for the murderers and accomplices in the plot to kill Barnett. Greco accepted the murder contract in July 1914.

Greco's first idea was murder on the cheap.

Cardinale and Greco finally succeeded in hiring Russo and Di Paolo to do the job.

Russo was "very thin"...and Di Paolo "very fat."

"I told him the boys were too young," said Cardinale, "but he said he would give them some cocaine to snuff, and after a few snuffs they would do anything."[45]

Though, as a criminal, Greco could have obtained cocaine, it was also still freely available at pharmacies until the Harrison Act, passed in December 1914, took effect in 1915.

The New York Times of April 4, 1916 gives more insight into the unsuccessful attempts of Russo and Di Paolo and into the guys themselves.

Calmly asserting to the jury that he himself was a horse thief and a professional gunman, Carmine di Paolo, a young Italian of college training, testified ... that he went gunning for Barnet Baff ... not less than six times and that on one occasion he carried a poisoned dagger to accomplish his purpose if a bullet failed.

Di Paolo finally retired from the murder conspiracy, because the fee for which he undertook ... the "job" was too small - $75 – and the risk too great...

Di Paolo had a public school education and attended St. John's College at Fordham University for a year and a half.* Whatever education he had received, however, he said, could not withstand the influence of thieves, gamblers, and gunmen, who lured him into a life of crime.

Di Paolo ... only 21 years old, was well dressed, quick and deft in speech, but so easily angered that a question on cross-examination often sent him into a fury ...

He and his sixteen-year-old "pal," Carmello Russo were lured into the conspiracy by Joseph Zafarone and Ipollito Greco ... After the fourth trip [to Washington Market] ... when he returned to Greco's saloon ... [Greco] swore at him for postponing the job ... Greco abused him in strong language because he did not let the "kid," meaning Russo, do the job, because he was under 16 and "wouldn't get the electric chair."

On the fifth trip ... Greco gave him what he called a cheese dagger ... "It was really an ice pick poisoned at the end. Greco told me that if circumstances were such that I could not conveniently shoot Baff I should stick him in the back with this knife and that would end him."

However, the Poultry King, Barnett Baff, was not to be felled with a cheese dagger. Di Paolo and Russo were replaced, as murderers for hire, by

---

* College education did not become common for the middle class until after World War II.

brothers Tony and Joseph Zaffarone. The Zaffarones would later distinguish themselves by the unrepentant, matter-of-fact way that they discussed the murder plot.

> One of their chief means of refreshing their memory was by reference to acts of grand larceny or burglary which they had committed near the times they were being questioned about. One of the Zafarano [sic] brothers, after admitting that he had been in various expeditions from "Little Italy" to the market to murder Baff, denied that they had been along on one specific occasion.
>
> "I know we were not there that day," he said, "because that night we were stealing horses. We stole six horses in Newark that night, and I am sure of it because that night Greko [sic] charged us $5 for keeping the horses in his stable and we made a big row because it was too much."[46]

However, the gunmen balked at a street level shooting. Their alternative idea was to hide a gunman in a loft directly across the street from Barnett's shop. A man, with a Winchester rifle, hid in the second story of Charlie Hawk's chicken market. (The rifle, silencer and box of cartridges were purchased for $26.50.). However, "too many persons came up and down the stairs, and the gunman declined to work from that position." A second attempt was made from Charlie Werner's loft. A three inch hole was drilled in the wall to hold the barrel of the rifle, but the gunman gave up after several days in which he did not see Barnett pass. Both Hawk and Werner had been convicted in the Poultry Trust Case[47] though neither appears to have been one of the main conspirators in the murder plot.

Barnett was well aware of the enmity directed at him by his business rivals. A short time before his death, he told his business ally, A.T. Pearson, "they are going to get me and they are going to get you. Watch what I tell you."[48]

After the shooting-from-a-loft plan did not work out, reconnaissance started for a street level attempt. The Summer of 1914 saw a total of six trips to West Washington Market, to murder Barnett, by Sicilian gangsters of Harlem's Little Italy. During this time, Barnett acquired a police guard from the Charles Street Police Station, in Greenwich Village, and by the end of August 1914 attempts on his life were suspended.[49]

Nothing changed for the members of the Live Poultry Dealers Protective Association. They were struggling in the hyper-competitive conditions created by Barnett. They feared for the effect on their businesses during the coming holidays.

Thanksgiving, Christmas and New Year's were potentially their most profitable time. They began to question their leadership: Where was the hoped for legal remedy? What had happened to their contributions? Could they have them back, please? "At that stage, it is believed, many more than the original twelve conspirators were made acquainted with the true plan to get rid of Baff."[50]

The design was coming into focus. There was mounting pressure to act. When the plotters discovered that Barnett's police guard had been withdrawn, it was time to commit murder. The kosher retailers had motive and means and in the crowded market place, two days before Thanksgiving, they had opportunity. Barnett could be brilliant and independent in business, but he could be neither independent of legal protection nor immortal.

Tuesday, November 24, 1914

On this day, two days before Thanksgiving, Barnett was up before the sun his mind on the busy season of the poultry business. He came downstairs from the second floor of his carved-mahogany festooned brownstone and down the stoop. His house, 76 West 120th Street, was on a tree lined block just off the fashionable residential square surrounding Mount Morris Park. The area, developed in the waning decades of the nineteenth century, was increasingly an Eastern European Jewish community. Unlike the Jewish Lower East Side and the tenement blocks of East Harlem, this was a community for those who had been successful in entering the American upper middle class.

Harry Baff, Barnett's junior partner, and his wife, Rose, lived around the corner and down the block at 100 West 119th Street. As befitted the junior partner, this was an apartment building, not a private house, and at the corner of commercial Lenox Avenue. As was the custom of the time, Barnett's three younger, unmarried children lived at home.

Either by subway, elevated train, or private car, Barnett made his last trip from his lovely home in Harlem to the wind swept, wave battered rectangle, in the Hudson River, on which West Washington Market was built. In his office, pasted to his wall, were clippings from trade papers. One read:

> "March 20-Baff under ban ... B. Baff & Son were boycotted by the buyers' organization of Live Poultry Dealers' Protective Association. At a meeting he was asked to give up distributing markets, of which he has four. Baff refused and he was boycotted.

Then in Barnett's handwriting, "I refused their demands. I have not lost nerve yet. I will fight to a finish."[51] Barnett's determination was written, in Barnett's hand, on Barnett's wall.

Harry, his son and partner, was there in West Washington Market too. Another son, William, in his early twenties and 17 year old son Isadore (later called Irving) worked for the business as well. However, it is not clear if and when these two younger sons were in the Market that day. Barnett's daughter, Etta, named in memory of his mother, Yetta, may have already worked for the business too.

It was the second day before Thanksgiving. The market was crowded with customers.

Crates of chickens and turkeys were piled high on every sidewalk, and hundreds of automobiles were in and around the market.

On any other day in the year except the second day before Christmas an automobile would have attracted attention, but ... the automobile in which the gunmen escaped could stand at Thirteenth Avenue and Gansevoort Street for an hour unnoticed. Also, the gunmen could dodge behind the piles of crates in running to their car.[52]

Barnett's business enemies were poised to act; saloon owner Ippolito Greco had his men lined up. In the Italian section of East Harlem, one of the murder conspirators hired a coffee-colored Fiat touring car from the Market Auto Garage at 435 East 104th Street. From the garage, a phone call was made to a local plumber and occasional chauffeur, Frank Ferrara, at his home at 224 East 107th Street. Ferrara was asked to pick up two gunmen on a corner near the garage. One of them was Giuseppe Arichiello with close ties to Harlem's Lupo Gang. The other may have been Gaetano Rina.[53]

Also along for the ride was one of the Jewish businessmen. This was risky, because of the potential to reveal the identity of one of the conspirators. However, it was done to oversee the process and lower the risk of another failed attempt at murder. Though he was going to kill a stranger for the money, Arichiello did ask the poultry dealer why Baff was being gotten out of the way. "He sells chickens cheap and makes us buy them high," answered the poultry man. "He has been ruining our business."[54] Just like the Sicilian gunman, the Jewish poultry dealer was committing murder for money.

Meanwhile, West Washington Market was busy with plotting as well as commerce. That morning, Antonio Cardinale, go-between for the poultrymen and the Italians, had been to the Market to see Jewish conspirator Abe Graff. Cardinale was there to say that "the job was to be done in the afternoon. Graff ... told him he would have everything ready" which would include warning the chief conspirators to stay clear of the action. One man left the market at 5pm and went to a saloon in Jersey City, New Jersey. He played pinochle with friends until 7pm, establishing an alibi for the time of the murder.[55]

Abe Graff also sought out Moses Rosenstein, a Market worker known as "Chicken Moe",

> "Moe, you're just the boy I'm looking for. You're the only man I've ever known who didn't back away from anybody who done you harm. Moe, this is what I want you to do. Should you see any one interfere with these fellows who are coming down here to put Baff away, you measure them so you'll be sure they fall."[56]

While Ferrara drove the gunmen downtown, Ippolito Greco, saloon owner and East Harlem contractor for hiring gangsters, went to West Washington Market to oversee his crew's work. Sometime horse thief Joseph Zaffarone and another criminal went to the Market to be lookouts.[57] It would be their job to signal if they saw the cops and to create a diversion if necessary, perhaps have the police arrest one of them for committing a petty crime. The lookouts could also mingle with the crowd after the murder to confuse witnesses with disinformation about the details of the crime,[58] like the license number of the getaway car.

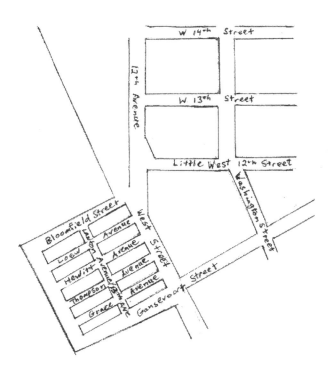

West Washington Market and Vicinity

It was afternoon when the gunmen drove into the market place. The cast was assembled. One of the Jewish conspirators supplied the gunmen with revolvers. One of the revolvers was nickel-plated; the other had a wooden handle and an extra long barrel. The poultry man who had ridden down to the market with the gunmen encouraged them to act. However, "they were unable to proceed with their work at once because detectives were discovered buying turkeys in the vicinity. After the coast was clear, Graff ... said he would call Baff out to answer a telephone call, thus bringing him within range of the assassins."[59]

Graff and another businessman/conspirator went into a saloon. Most likely it was the one at

> Thirteenth and Thompson Avenues,[*] directly across the latter thoroughfare from Baff's stall and next door in Thirteenth Avenue to the Brooklyn Poultry Company. It has glass doors opening into both of the avenues, and

---

[*] Early 20th Century maps show Thirteenth Avenue as a southern continuation of Twelfth Avenue in the West 20's. Officially, there is and was no Thirteenth Avenue as far south as West Washington Market. However, from the description of the murder, it becomes clear that the street being referred to as Thirteenth Avenue is named Lawton Avenue on century old maps.

any one standing in it can see Baff's business stand ... It would have been easy for one who knew Baff to observe him leave his place of business and then to point him out to the gunmen, who might be lurking behind any of the crates of poultry piled up on the sidewalks.[60]

The phone call to Barnett was probably placed from a wooden public phone booth in this saloon.

Late in the afternoon, Barnett's employee, George Levin, answered the black phone in B. Baff & Son. The voice on the other end spoke good English and asked for Barnett. He claimed to have "information about chicken thefts from Baff's Harlem market." This call verified Barnett's presence in his stall.[61]

Meanwhile, Ferrarra was keeping the motor running on the coffee-colored Fiat touring car. This was probably one of the exclusive U.S models manufactured by American Fiat, after 1912, in Poughkeepsie, New York. Fiat had moved manufacturing for the American Market to the United States to avoid paying tariffs. This was done at a time when the Federal Government's revenue came primarily from taxing imports. The modern income tax was not approved until 1913.

The Fiat driven by Ferrara was most likely a car that incorporated the electric self-starter that was invented, in 1912, to replace the hand crank. Though it was an open car, presumably the removable roof had been left on to obscure the identities of the passengers. Ferrarra "shifted his car three times in an effort to make escape easy." He was ultimately placed at Thirteenth Avenue near Gansevoort Street.[62]

> Within half an hour after the telephone call, some one stuck his head into Baff's door and said the dealer was wanted at a stand in Thirteenth Avenue not 100 feet from his place of business ... he accepted it without suspicion because it was not unusual for him to be called to any stand in the market to inspect poultry offered for sale.[63]

As Barnett crossed Thompson Avenue, Michael Garlich, whose stand was at 11 South Thirteenth Avenue, spoke to him briefly and then went into a coffee house. Next Barnett ran into Moe Rosenstein who raised his hat to him. This was a signal that Graff had asked Rosenstein to make.

The gunmen, walking behind Rosenstein, shot three times. "One bullet hit Baff in the chest, and passed through his heart. A second entered his left shoulder." It was almost 6:00 p.m.[64]

Barnett fell in front of the Brooklyn Poultry Company.

Adolph Danziger was in his stand nearby.

> He heard the shots fired. He ran out to the sidewalk and as he reached it a man carrying a revolver in one hand dashed by him within a foot of his face. Danziger, frightened, ran back into his stand as fast as he could and did not get a good look at the gunman.[65]

Five bank clerks who had been picking up turkeys at Danziger's, were standing outside

> When they heard two revolver shots a short distance up Thirteenth Avenue. They turned in time to see the two gunmen fleeing toward them, one running on the sidewalk on which they were standing and the other running in the street ... the man on the sidewalk ... was shorter than his companion, and though apparently well nourished had a white, pinched face, indicating, in the opinion of the police, that he was a cocaine user ... although he ran away from the body of Baff ... he looked backward while he ran to see if he was being pursued. He carried a nickel-plated revolver in his right hand, which was partly extended in front of him ... it seemed ... [he] was ready to shoot any one who tried to stop him.[66]

Abraham Lowenstein, an officer of the Brooklyn Poultry Company, saw Barnett fall "and caught a glimpse of the backs of the fleeing gunmen." "Lowenstein said he saw two men running and started in pursuit, but one of them ... Moses Rosenstein ... got in his way at Thompson and Thirteenth."

Rosenstein diverted Lowenstein to Baff's stand where Barnett was lying on the ground. Barnett had been moved by some combination of the first people to arrive on the scene after the shooting: Patrolman Dennis Sullivan, Isadore Blatt, Samuel Blatt[*], and Harry Baff.[67] When Harry saw that his father was dead, he collapsed and was sent home in a taxi.[68]

From their truck, piano movers, who had come to the Market for their Thanksgiving turkeys, "heard two shots and saw two men jump into an automobile in front of them and drive away." "The gunmen reached their automobile at about the same time and hurriedly climbed in as the chauffeur threw in the clutch. A moment later the automobile had whizzed around the corner into

---

[*] Though Isadore and Samuel's last name is given as Blatt, this is probably a mistake. Harry Baff is more likely to have been accompanied by his brother, Isadore Baff, and his uncle, Samuel Baff than an unrelated Isadore and Samuel.

Gansevoort Street" and continued east to West Street. At this point, the larger man who had been running in the street threw away his revolver. Ferrarra drove the two gunmen to a downtown elevated train station "into which they disappeared."[69] (The closest station was at 9th Avenue and 14th Street, six blocks from where the car had been parked.). As the car fled, smoke from its tailpipe may have obscured its license plate.[70]

* * *

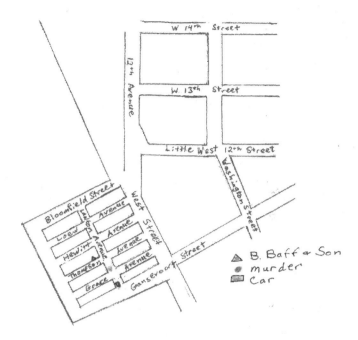

Murder!

After diverting Lowenstein, Rosenstein rejoined Graff. They went to a saloon, where they met Joe Cohen. "Graff said, 'Well, we got him that time,' and Joe pushed him aside and replied, 'Don't tell me anything about it'." Eventually Cardinale, who had been hanging around the market, rejoined Rosenstein and Graff. They went to Graff's stand. Cardinale and Rosenstein each "took a turkey to disarm suspicion and walked out of the market without attracting attention." Around 7:00 p.m., someone placed a call to the man playing pinochle in Jersey City. It was done from a public pay phone to make the call untraceable. The card player returned to Manhattan.[71]

Dr. Kellogg from New York Hospital, then located on West 15th and 16th Streets, declared that Barnett had died instantly.[72] Barnett finished his American journey under the care of the oldest hospital in New York City, second oldest in the nation. Barnett Baff, the man, was buried soon after. Barnett Baff, the murder case, had just taken on a protean life of its own.

Barnett's life was the story of one man with outsize ambition. His murder case, on the other hand, became a morass of push and pull between the aspirations of many stakeholders. Even within the government, the New York City Police, the Manhattan District Attorney and the officials of New York State had different axes to grind. The Sicilian gangsters cared nothing for the Jews. Each Jewish conspirator wanted to save himself as did the stool pigeon turned "investigator" Philip Musica. Meanwhile, Barnett's wife and children had to live on without the driving force of Barnett, but with the chaos that came in the wake of his dead body.

A Long Finish to 1914

The evening after the murder, the scene shifted to the Italian section of East Harlem. The Sicilian gunmen and accomplices were reunited at Ippolito Greco's saloon. It was time to pay them off though not without contention.

Abe Graff was the bag man. He got $500 from Joseph Cohen and delivered it to Greco. Greco in turn paid gunman Arichiello $100, but Chauffeur Ferrara only $90. Ferrara claimed that he had been promised $100 too. He also threatened to expose the plot. The brawl that ensued was enough for someone to call the police who didn't think much of it at the time. When Greco saw the attention being attracted by Ferrara, he gave him the additional ten dollars.[73]

The Sicilians continued to ask for more money. Joseph Cohen eventually came across with an additional thousand dollars. Graff delivered it to one of the hired guns on the corner of Lenox Avenue and 142nd Street. In addition to a series of payments from Cohen, Cardinale received help opening a chicken market in Brooklyn[74] before he fled to Italy.*

The morning after the big, tempestuous payoff at Greco's saloon was Barnett's bleak funeral. Then he was buried in Brooklyn. His gravesite, acquired through Temple Anshe Bialystock, is in Washington Cemetery. Unlike Brooklyn's prestigious garden cemetery, Greenwood, Washington Cemetery is a utilitarian place. It is crowded with grave stones with patches of grass in between. Today, Barnett's stone is joined by those of his brother, Samuel, his wife, Fannie, their son, William, their son, Harry, and Harry's wife, Rose. The family plot is surrounded by a low, gated fence. An elevated portion of the F train bisects the cemetery on it's way to and from Coney Island.

On November 26, 1914, Thanksgiving Day, Washington Cemetery was more sparsely covered with grave stones. The F train was decades in the future. As Barnett had founded his family in

---

* According to Ferrara, the final tally was $250 each to Carmine di Paolo, to the unknown gunman and to himself. Each of the Zaffarano's received $300. Arichiello, though firing the fatal shot, only received $100. However, he was incarcerated about 3 months after the murder. Perhaps he missed out on later payoffs. Greco received $1000 outright, but also skimmed some of the payments to his contract labor. About $2000 more went to Cardinale and perhaps other go-betweens. (NY Times 2/13/1916)

America, he was also the first to be buried in his family plot. The ground was cold even if the grass was still green from the previous summer. Barnett's family was at his grave site, using the strength acquired from hefting crates of chickens, to bury his coffin with shovels full of dirt. It was, and is, the Jewish tradition to bury one's own dead, sometimes literally, sometimes with merely symbolic action.

Afterwards, back in Manhattan, a distraught Harry Baff spoke to the press despite having been asked, by the District Attorney's Office, not to do so. At this point, the press wondered which of four groups of enemies had gone after Barnett. Harry did not think that his father had been killed by members of the gang who had robbed his father's store in Harlem and seen five of their members go to Sing Sing Prison for the crime. Nor did he think that his father had been murdered by chicken handlers who were fired when chickens had been found to be fed gravel. Harry opined that there was no reason for the old Poultry Trust to have committed the murder, but pinned it on Barnett's retail rivals who "wanted him removed from the field of competition. [Because] He was too big and too strong for them."[75]

Meanwhile, the Mayor of New York City, John Purroy Mitchel, and a shocked public deplored the murder in their midst. The business climate was such that businessmen were considered to have a duty to make money. Starting with a spectacular run-on sentence, The New York Times of November 26, 1914 editorialized, drawing parallels to the recent public slaying of Herman Rosenthal.

> The murder of Barnet Baff, the poultry dealer, has shocked this community even more than the murder of Rosenthal, the gambler, a crime to which, in the police view, it bears a strong resemblance, with this difference, that, while Rosenthal was the very scum of society, Baff, so far as is known, was an upright and law-abiding man, who had conducted his business honorably and done no more than his duty in incurring the avowed enmity of some of his rivals in trade. If those rivals are not implicated in this cowardly assassination, except in the inevitable suspicions of Baff's acquaintances, they will do well to publish the proofs of their innocence as quickly as possible. This is not a case in which the excellent rule that every man should be considered innocent until he has been proved guilty is likely to have much weight in the public mind.

The indications that here is another gunmen murder, a killing in a public thoroughfare by hired assassins, are very strong. The police have taken up the matter with energy and there is scarcely a doubt that they will soon run the actual murderers to earth ...

That all or nearly all the members of the Poultry Men's Union are responsible for the instigation of this crime is incredible. Resort to murder because of trade enmities is very rare in this country. But a man has been killed in circumstances which throw suspicion upon a body of marketmen, and it will be to the advantage of that body to render all help to the authorities in bringing the guilty persons to justice.

The plea for those familiar with West Washington Market to come forward was much more than rhetorical flourish. In the days immediately following the murder, no one on intimate terms with the market place would speak. West Washington Market was emerging in the public eye as a gang infested operation with intimidation of those who were law abiding. Police Commissioner Arthur Woods said of it,

"Everything is in a mess over there, and we want to find out just what made the mess. We are going to get at the truth of all these reports of thugs and blackmailers and crooks and we are going to find out who are the undesirables and why they are in the market. Then we are going in to clean house and make the Washington Market a decent place for honest businessmen. We have found out a great deal already, one thing being that almost every one in the market is afraid to talk. I warn the undesirables in the market to get out at once, because we are going after them with the full force of the Police Department."[76]

Woods had only been Commissioner since April serving under reform Republican mayor John Purroy Mitchel and modernizing the police force. This was the moment when the police started to receive professional training. They were deployed to break up gangs and to destroy their influence on labor unions. Under Commissioner Woods, the police would also engage in extensive disaster preparedness and contingency planning.[*] They would not only be a force against criminals, but protectors of public well being. They were dubbed "super-police."[77]

---

[*] Part of this effort was figuring out how to feed the population of New York City in the event of the usual supply lines being disrupted. Barnett's knowledge of the various aspects of the marketplace would have been useful to Commissioner Wood's effort and Barnett, in turn, would have used whatever he learned to his competitive advantage. Sadly, Barnett was no more.

Based on the Baff case, Commissioner Woods set up a school of identification for automobiles. The plan was to "use one hundred different types of automobiles with which every policeman must familiarize himself." The training ran for three hours a day for twenty-eight days.[78]

While the police did the legwork, the Manhattan District Attorney's office questioned witnesses to build the legal case against the murderers, both gunmen and conspirators. Walter R. Deuel, the Assistant District Attorney (A.D.A) assigned to the murder, would go on to a long and pivotal involvement with the case. A.D.A. William De Ford, of the Poultry Trust prosecution, was called upon to assist with knowledge of the poultry industry. Charles S. Whitman was still District Attorney. By this time, the Rosenthal Case/corrupt cop Charles Becker prosecution had catapulted him to prominence. Whitman was Governor Elect of New York State, set to take office on January 1, 1915. With less than two weeks remaining as D.A., Whitman had turned over most of his duties to Acting District Attorney Delehanty. However, when it looked like the Baff case might reach a quick conclusion, Whitman, ever the ambitious politician, took charge of it.[79]

The presence of Whitman led to repeated concerns about cooperation between the police and the D.A.'s office. He had not only pinned Rosenthal's murder on a policeman, but had been critical, at the time, of the police department in general. However, the D.A.'s office and the Police Department conferred frequently and nothing came of the rumor that Whitman would complain to Mayor Mitchel about the cops.

In fact, the police were working effectively on the Baff Case. The cops were doggedly watching suspects that they lacked the proof to arrest. They were bringing in people for questioning, bringing in suspects on old warrants and concealed weapons charges. They had James Moore, who had done dirty work for Jacob and Joseph Cohen, turn state's evidence. Brothers Jacob and Joseph Cohen were arrested on an old assault charge and each held on $25,000 bail. They had hired James Moore for one of the assaults on Barnett's ally, A.T. Pearson.

Carl Rettich, bartender in his father's Hoboken saloon, brought in guns that he claimed were the murder weapons and confessed to being a go-between for the plotters and James Moore. He did in fact pay an attorney for Moore's defense.

The police rounded up gangsters from West Washington Market and literally said, "Beat it." They worked with stool pigeons and around the many private detectives hired by Harry Baff and by two different groups of market men.[80] They even submitted to being arrested themselves:

> Inspector Faurot sent two detectives to Weehawken with instructions to dress as toughs and pick up gossip among the chicken handlers in the freight yards and saloons. The detectives made up for their parts and within a few hours were posing as loiterers in Weehawken. They were soon on terms of familiarity with the more talkative chicken handlers. But in making his plans Inspector Faurot neglected to notify the Weehawken police, and Weehawken detectives pounced upon them as vagrants. They did not wish to make their identity known in public, so, protesting, they were taken to the Weehawken Police Headquarters. There they made themselves known and received the apologies of their captors.[81] *

---

* Inspector Joseph Faurot was the fingerprints expert of the

Harry Baff was confident in the police.

"The police are working on exactly the right lines and I am sure they will soon have the murderers of my father in jail.

I have given the police much information bearing on the case and they have acted on it capably. The net has been thrown out and it is now being drawn in. When it is pulled all the way in you will find that the big fish of the murder conspiracy will be caught in it. I hear from the police everyday and know that they are making progress. Nothing shows on the surface yet but you must remember that we are dealing with a very clever set of men and have to proceed cautiously. If we make a misstep now and arrest the wrong man or let our plans become public, the whole investigation may fall through.

But have no fears about the results of the case. When we do act openly we must act with a rush and nab all of the murderers and conspirators at once. We are not quite prepared to close in on the whole crowd and if we got one or two now, the remainder

---

New York City Police Department. He had studied the technique in Europe and then had demonstrated its usefulness to the Police Department. The arrest of his men, investigating the Baff Case, may have given him the idea for a subsequent prank. On vacation in Jacksonville, Florida, Faurot and a colleague introduced themselves to the local police by acting suspiciously, getting arrested and then revealing their true identities. According to the New York Times of February 20, 1916, the Jacksonville police "retaliated by entertaining the visiting crime-hunters."

would get away. None of the men we want will get away. I am sure of that."[82]

The National Association of Car Lot Poultry Shippers, Barnett's far-flung allies in the South and West, offered a reward of $200 for the arrest and conviction of Barnett's murderers. However, for financial reasons, the group voted to discontinue A.T. Pearson as its special New York City representative.[83]

The general public had its say too. Outraged New Yorkers were invited to a meeting, of the recently formed Citizens' Protective League, at Cooper Union. Here the police and commissioner Woods did come in for criticism, but there were also complaints from the police themselves on the rules that they had to follow. Fannie Baff, Harry Baff and his sister, Etta Baff, attended the meeting. They had been back in West Washington Market, at B. Baff and Son, since a bare six days after the murder. Harry, fearing his fathers enemies, was accompanied everywhere by six body guards and applied for a gun permit.[84] His brother, William Baff, got a gun too.

The District Attorney's office convened a grand jury to hear evidence in the murder case.

Harry and seventeen year old Isadore (later Irving) Baff* were among those testifying. Every day the New York Times had one or two articles reporting the latest developments. As late as December 29, 1914, indictments leading to the conviction of "the men higher-up" were expected, but the next day the indictments were postponed. Whitman's stated intent was to include more of the guilty men. He also wanted to keep the Grand Jury in session rather than having them return indictments against a few conspirators, be dismissed and then be replaced by a new Grand Jury which would start hearing evidence all over again.[85] Whitman departed for his swearing in as Governor. Incoming D.A. Perkins was expected to personally continue working on indictments.

---

* "Isadore Baff, the dead man's youngest son, was also a witness before the Grand Jury. While not so well acquainted with his father's business as is his older brother, Harry, he is better acquainted with what might be called the market "underworld." He had charge of his father's trucking for some time, and this work put him in touch with the handlers at the Jersey freight yards. He knows them and is more or less familiar with conditions among them. For this reason he was able to explain many things that Harry Baff, when he is called as a witness, will not be able to touch upon." (New York Times 12/24/1914)

The Power of the Press

From the time of the murder until the beginning of 1915, the national press indulged the public fascination with murder and with the evils of life in the big city. The *Fort Worth Star Telegram* of December 20 had this front page headline: "$270 Price of Murder in New York". The Duluth News – Tribune, quipped, "The Rosenthal and Baff cases in New York indicated that it is cheaper to hire murderers than to hire lawyers to defend them. "[86]

The Idaho Statesman reported that New York City needed reform to "free itself from the deadly grasp of its demon."[87] The Baltimore Evening Sun said, "The modern city is the natural jungle and refuge of social outlaws, as the forest and the mountains were at an earlier period ... in every large city ... anarchy lurks beneath civilization."[88] The still largely agrarian country was expressing its fear of massed lower classes.

All over the City, all over the nation, Barnett's murder was described and deplored. It was also being illustrated, e.g in the Tampa Morning Tribune. Photoengravings depicted Barnett and Fanny, Fanny alone and Fanny with her children.

The grieving family was, through no fault of their own, a publicly displayed family.*

Eventually, the national notoriety of the murder would affect the prosecution of the case, but that would be more than four years in the making.

---

* Though generally of a matter of fact mind set, it was difficult for me to see the pictures. They were poorly reproduced on the library data base, but still I could distinguish the familiar Isadore standing between his brothers. I wondered if he had decided to be called Irving to restore a modicum of privacy.

And Then Nothing Happened

After January 1, 1915, the case dropped out of the headlines. While it had been one thing to nurture suspicions and another to gather evidence, it was quite something else to be able to convict anyone in court.   Pending additional witnesses, those who were being held were let go or, like the Cohen brothers, had their bail reduced to something which they could pay.[89]

The lack of action was noticed. On January 28th, this brief letter to the editor appeared in the New York Times:

> Have we, the public, a right to ask why the Baff murder case has sunk into oblivion? Was no one found guilty, or were there too many found guilty? Was there no evidence, or was there too much evidence? Was some one afraid or was someone paid?
>
> Are the gunmen an overestimated power, or is the strength back of them so great that we are afraid to face them? F.D.L.

Though it is likely that the D.A.'s office had explained the postponement of action to Harry Baff, it did not sit well with the Baff family.   Charles Becker's conviction in the   Rosenthal Case had shown that it was easy to blame the police for public ills. Additionally, young Isadore (Irving) Baff was no friend to the police. In 1913, he and a friend had been arrested for insulting a cop in Central Park. They had been dragged into Night Court and fined by a judge who had trouble keeping a straight face as he contemplated the big complainant cop and the scrawny teenage boys[*].

On the evening of Tuesday, June 15, 1915, the Baff brothers acted out. William, who exhibited life-long unstable tendencies, started it off. He was in a crowd of people gathered around two police detectives, Namoli and Confrey, at Lenox Avenue and 116th Street, near his home in Harlem. The plainclothes cops were questioning some youths in a car about the whereabouts of a suspect in a crime wholly unrelated to Barnett's murder. The detectives might well have been seeking the drug suspect who had shot Officer Confrey's partner[†], on the previous evening, and escaped into Central Park.[90]

> According to the detectives, [William] Baff presently pushed towards them and demanded to know what business they had

---

[*] See Appendix C for details.
[†] Confrey's partner, Detective John Caspers, survived.

questioning men in the street. They told him to mind his business ... he hit Namoli over the head with an umbrella and ran into a haberdashery.

Confrey followed ... Baff drew a revolver and threatened him until the detective showed his shield and warned the young man to put up the weapon which he has a permit to carry since his life was threatened after the murder of his father. Baff was taken to the West 123rd Street Police Station. He sent for his brother, Isidor, who lives with him at 76 West 120th Street, and for Harry, another brother, living at 100 West 119th Street.

William is 22 years old. The elder brothers, who are 31 and 30, respectively, became so abusive in the station that Lieutenant Fitzgerald ordered the policeman to put them out, while William cried, "Why don't you get the murderers of my father instead of bothering us?"

The elder Baffs loitered around the station house and such a crowd collected that they were warned to move on. When they refused, and kept up loud talking and criticism, Lieutenant Fitzgerald had them arrested, too. William was charged with interfering with an officer and with assaulting Namoli. His brothers were held on charges of disorderly conduct.[91]

One imagines Fannie or Etta Baff calling a lawyer to bail them out in the morning so that they could get back to work in West Washington Market.

It is unknown whether the Times made a clerical error in giving Isadore's age as 31 or Isadore was being a wise guy with the police. He was only 18.

Elsewhere Things Happened

In 1915, World War I raged on in Europe and on the seas where Germany sank neutral American ships. Albert Einstein published his *General Theory of Relativity.* The one millionth Model T rolled off the Ford Motors assembly line. Brooklyn, New York got its first subway line. Woodrow Wilson became the first President to attend a World Series game.

On July 30th, former policeman Charles Becker went to the electric chair, at Sing Sing prison, for masterminding the murder of gambling house owner Herman Rosenthal. This was, as mentioned before, the case that gave D.A. Charles Whitman the popularity to run for Governor. *New Yorker* writer Andy Logan wrote a book about the murder of Rosenthal and the prosecution of Becker.[92] In it, she makes a strong case against the justice of Whitman's prosecution of Becker. While her case may be flawed, it does include two irrefutable facts. First, the initial conviction of Becker was thrown out on appeal showing the case to be weak. Second, Becker was effectively denied his final appeal. This breach of due process was caused when Becker's last appeal for clemency had to be made to New York State Governor Whitman who was clearly biased against Becker from his experience as the District Attorney who prosecuted Becker. The situation was unprecedented, but instead of letting the Lieutenant Governor hear Becker's appeal or temporarily staying the execution, Whitman proceeded with Becker's electrocution. Whitman's drive to punish rather than to observe the fine points of the law may have also influenced the prosecution of the Baff murder case.

February and October 1915 brought two other seemingly unrelated developments. On February 25th, the young Sicilian gangster Giuseppe Arichiello was arrested in Harlem's Little Italy. He was convicted and incarcerated on a gun charge.

On October 7th, Ippolito Greco, saloon owner and supplier of gangster labor, was shot to death, on East 108th Street, in Harlem's Little Italy. Soon after, his relative who was familiar with his endeavors, Gaetano Lo Monte, was also killed. These murders gave the police some grist for their mill even though they may have resulted from rivalry between Sicilian and Neopolitan gangs rather than the Baff Case.

Police Commissioner Woods had pulled the pieces together when he said,

> "It's a fine thing, you know, when a detective catches a murderer the day after the crime, seizes him around the neck, and shakes him before the public, saying, 'here's your man;' but very often such sensational police work is not evidence of the best detective work. The best detective work is done when the men dig and dig and dig on a tough case and hang on until they get the whole thing cleared up. Such work is not sensational, though, and the detectives often do not get credit for what they do, because they finish after the public has lost interest in the case. Now this Baff murder is one of the toughest cases that we have ever had. We can't do anything sensational, perhaps, but we are digging and digging and digging and we will hang on until we get all of the murderers."[93]

Woods statement is still an apt description of the difference between a good detective story and a real detective story.

There was one clearly positive development, in August: The murderers' getaway car was found in an East Harlem garage. However, the police worked on this development quietly, without publicity. By the end of 1915, a year of police digging and connecting the pieces that they dug up, Barnett's murder was poised to return to the headlines.

1916: The Year of the Sicilians

About a year had passed since the letter to the New York Times complaining of inaction on Barnett's Murder. On February 10, 1916, the story finally returned to the news. It began again with the wisdom of Commissioner Woods:

> "The newspapers will soon drop this case and the public will forget it, but the police will keep plugging at it for months and months until it is cleared up. I can't tell how long it will take, but sooner or later we will get to the bottom of every thing. The case is on our files as unfinished, and it will remain so until it is finished."

> So spoke Commissioner Arthur Woods a few weeks after two gunmen killed Barnet Baff ... Months passed, the newspapers did drop the case, but yesterday afternoon ... a young Italian stood in Police Headquarters and confessed that he drove the automobile in which the slayers of Baff escaped, and named as the gunman a man who is serving a sentence in Nappanock Reformatory for carrying a revolver, and the high-power coffee-colored murder car that the young Italian drove stood outside Headquarters.[94]

The car had been found, then the driver and sometime plumber Frank Ferrara. When the police were investigating Ippolito Greco's murder, they tied the fight in his saloon on Wednesday,

November 25, 1914 to Barnett's murder. This helped them identify Ferrara as the driver of the hired getaway car. He, in turn, had fingered Giuseppe Arichiello, also known as Arcola, Circalla and Artilla. Though Ferrara was described as making a full confession, he would not or could not identify the second gunman.

The police had Giuseppe Arichiello transferred to police headquarters. They brought in Antonio and Joseph Zaffarano. (Antonio was out on bail on a charge of pimping for a minister's daughter.). The police also held Carmine di Paolo, who had quit the murder conspiracy, as a material witness.[95]

*   *   *

It was the hope of the police to follow the trail of Barnett's murderers to the men higher up who had paid for the crime. "It is believed that if the case is cleared up completely a score or more of men will stand charged with murder in the first degree." The police had signed warrants to arrest these conspirators and they had them under surveillance. However they lacked the evidence to convict them in court. They hoped to, in time, get valuable information from the poultry dealers who contributed to the murder fund thinking it would be put to other use.[96]

There was one major obstacle to getting the evidence to convict the instigators of Barnett's murder. Greco had been the go-between for the gangsters and the business men, but Greco had been killed, in his own stable, for what he knew, perhaps specifically for what he knew of Barnett's murder. The authorities wouldn't have Greco's testimony, but they would keep piecing together the information they could get. For example they received some help from a minor Mata Hari:

> A young woman who is related to Barnet Baff's family, and who, shortly after the murder, was courted by a man related to one of the chief instigators of the crime. This man, innocent of any part in the murder plot, knew some of its inside facts, and in the ardency of his courtship, it is said, imparted his knowledge to the woman, who wishing to avenge the death of her relative, gave the information to the police.[97]

*   *   *

The day after the murder returned to the headlines, Arichiello reenacted it for the police in Manhattan District Attorney Swann's office. The next day, police detectives and photographers took Ferrara to West Washington Market. He showed how he had positioned the car on the day of the murder. Then "acting as stage manager, assigned the detectives to act successively the parts played on the day of the murder by the 10 men who were there when the shots were fired. Police photographers took pictures of this realistic reproduction of the crime for use in making clear the geography and the action to a jury."[98]

The next day, Ferrara was expressing regret and telling the sad story of his life. "I wish I had broken both of my legs before I started out with that car," he declared. As a boy, Ferrara had been placed in an orphanage. (This might have been because his parents were dead or because they were alive but unable to care for him.). He had been befriended by philanthropist Evert Jansen Wendell.

> "Mr. Wendell gave me a start in life and got me my first job ... and for years I went absolutely straight. This is the first trouble I ever got into. I am married and have two children. But I got to going to Greko's [sic] saloon in Harlem because all of the other boys I knew went there, and just about the time Greko offered me $250 to pull off the

Baff murder I was out of a job and in debt, so I took the job."[99]

Mr. Wendell had been persuasive in getting Ferrara to cooperate with the authorities and provide a full confession.

Soon Ferrara was identifying Carmelo Russo, a.k.a. Charlie Ross, as one of the lookouts for the murderers. After trying to find Russo, the police had realized that he was in Elmira Reformatory for committing robbery. However, it turned out that while Russo was initially in on the murder plot, he was in jail, for burglary, on November 24, 1914 and another gunman took his place. Still Russo was casually willing to assert, "I would 'a been there sure, if I hadn't been locked up the day before." Arichiello I.D.'d another lookout, Joseph Zaffarano, who cursed him in Italian for doing so. On February 22nd Arichiello, Joseph Zaffarano and Ferrara were indicted.[100]

Ferrara pointed the way to plotter, go-between and paymaster Antonio Cardinale. However, the police discovered that Cardinale had fled to Italy where he was serving as a Corporal in the Italian Army on the Albanian frontier.[101] Now the District Attorney had another obstacle to proving his case against Barnett's murderers: Italy did not, at that time, allow its citizens to be tried in foreign courts.

*   *   *

At this point, the Baff family was back in the news briefly. Barnett, for all his business savvy and legal maneuvering, had not made a will. Eventually his assets were appraised and divided by the court. His children got equal shares and widow, Fannie, got about 50% more. The net estate was $76,392 at a time when the average worker earned less than $1000 a year. About 35 years before, Barnett had arrived in New York City with nothing. Now his children owned a piece of the City.

Barnett's wealth was in businesses and real estate with only $332 in a bank account. This was before the New Deal made bank accounts safe by requiring FDIC insurance. Real estate carried other risks, but Barnett's exposure was diversified as to location.* More than half the estate ($44,238) was

---

* 76 West 120 Street, 526-528 East Eightieth Street, 356 Johnson Avenue, Brooklyn, 10 South Crest Avenue, Arverne (Queens), a piece of land in Hamels, Rockaway (Queens), New

Barnett's two thirds interest in B. Baff and Son.[*] The future success of this business would most likely rest with his sole partner, Harry Baff.

*   *   *

Giuseppe Arichiello's trial began on April 3, 1916. Assistant District Attorney O'Malley opened with a two pronged statement. He would prove that Arichiello was guilty of murder. He also planned to prove that there had been a conspiracy to commit the murder, at least 3 months before it happened, with a fund collected for that purpose by persons not yet known.

Carmine di Paolo and Carmello Russo testified as to their involvement in the early stages of the plot as well as the involvement of Greco, a murder fund and Joseph and Jacob Cohen. Another of the prosecution's witnesses was Phillip Luporte, a bartender in Greco's saloon. He was unexpectedly jailed for perjury. He had previously sworn to witnessing the payoff of the Baff

---

York Times, 3/28/1916

[*] The business is listed at four locations: 62 Thompson Avenue, West Washington Market, 417 East 109th Street, East Harlem and 1834 Webster Avenue, The Bronx, and the previously noted 526-528 East Eightieth Street.

murderers, but when Luporte was called as a witness, he was uncooperative.

> As soon as he sat down in the witness chair he winked at the defendant, which Assistant District Attorney O'Malley was quick to observe. The prosecutor asked Luporte point blank why he winked at Arichiello and Luporte shifted his gaze to the window and mumbled, "No, I didn't wink."
>
> When examined as to the sworn statement he made ... before trial ... Luporte showed a total loss of memory on every essential point. The best he would do in response to many of the questions ... was to reply with a shake of his head. "Maybe yes and maybe no."...
>
> It was Luporte's reluctance to testify definitely as to Arichiello's presence on the Baff gunning trips that finally caused Justice Shearn to commit him for perjury.[102]

The next day, Arichiello, himself, recanted what he'd said before. The police had taken his confession; he'd repeated it to District Attorney Swann; he'd signed a confession; he and his defense attorney had agreed on a strategy. Then, Arichiello threw it all out claiming police brutality and a forced confession. He used police intimidation to explain his confession to the D.A. and his signing of his confession in a language that he claimed to be unable to read. Arichiello insisted that he did not murder Barnett.

After a brief character witness for Arichiello, A.D.A. O'Malley had witnesses to say that Arichiello matched the description of one of the murderers. At the summation, defense attorney William G. Keir pointed out that it was unfair to convict Arichiello on the testimony of Carmine di Paolo. It was inappropriate that though originally part of the murder conspiracy, di Paolo had been granted immunity from prosecution by the District Attorney's office. Mr. Keir "said it would be a gross injustice to allow such a man freedom and to send Arichiello, 'who was nothing but a poor rat without any semblance of brains,' to the electric chair."

In his summing up, A.D.A. O'Malley defended giving di Paolo immunity. He characterized the prosecution of Arichiello as "an opening wedge with which the District Attorney hoped to reach the men higher up ... We will never get the men higher up in this conspiracy until we first get the men lower down," he said.[103]

In his charge to the jury, Judge Shearn had praise for the work of the police and the district attorney. On Arichiello's claim of coerced confessions, he said that to believe that would involve believing in a conspiracy involving the interpreters and District Attorney Swann as well as the police. He said of Barnett's murder, "Such a crime strikes at the very heart of our civilization."[104]

After deliberating for six hours, the jury found Arichiello guilty of first degree murder. The jurors were reluctant to send a 21 year old to the electric chair when he might have been coerced by the older members of the conspiracy. They asked Judge Shearn if they could find Arichiello guilty, but recommend clemency. However, this was not a legal option.

Arichiello took the verdict calmly, but his sister-in-law, Mrs. Anna Arichiello, did not. She cursed out the detectives who heard Arichiello's confession and screamed to all, "You sent an innocent man to the electric chair."[105]

District Attorney Swann thought that the conviction of Arichiello might scare Ferrara or the Zaffarones into revealing the identities of the men higher up. While he thought that Arichiello was just a hired gun, he had a different opinion of the

three others who had been arrested. He thought
that they would have insisted on knowing more
details of the plot to give themselves more
bargaining power.[106]

Frank Ferrara's trial began on April 11, 1916
with both Judge Shearn presiding and A.D.A.
O'Malley prosecuting again. This time, Carmine di
Paolo's testimony brought more drama to the
proceedings. He was questioned closely by defense
attorney Caesar Barra about being an informer.
When asked to tell to whom he had talked about
the Baff murder conspiracy, before he talked to the
police, he did not want to answer. Judge Shearn
insisted. He finally replied,

> "That name I would not like to tell. I could
> not give out any name implicating—"

> He stopped and looked around the court
> room with a quick shifting gaze, after which
> he turned on Mr. Barra and exclaimed in
> anger:

> "You are asking me to sit on the electric
> chair. There are criminals of the gang sitting
> around the court. I'll tell you the truth. I'm
> the real informer in this case. I held it too
> long. I don't care what becomes of me now."

> Di Paolo admitted that he "squealed," but he
> said he did so to shield himself because he

knew that Joseph Zarafone [sic] ... intended to "put it all" on him.

"They were going to frame me ... before I could prove I was an innocent man."

As to his own share in the gunning expeditions ... " If I had refused ... they would have gunned me up."[107]

While Di Paolo described intimidation, Phillip Luporte, the reluctant witness at Arichiello's trial, was forthcoming on this occasion. His previous incarceration in the Tombs was probably persuasive. Luporte testified to witnessing the payoff of Arichiello, Ferrara and the Zaffarone brothers while he was bartending in Ippolito Greco's saloon.

The next day saw yet another reversal. Frank Ferrara, who had confessed and directed a reenactment of the murder in West Washington Market, recanted. Like Arichiello, he claimed that the police had beaten his confession out of him. He related that Greco had asked him to take a sick friend to the hospital. Under Greco's direction and with the two gunmen as passengers, he had driven to West Washington Market.

> When they reached the market ... he was directed to wait a few minutes. Not long after he heard what he thought was an explosion. Greco and the two men ran toward the car, jumped in and yelled to him to go as fast as he could.

> "I asked Greco what was that shooting that I had heard ... and Greco told me to forget about the shooting and go ahead."[108]

Besides denying any knowledge of the Baff murder conspiracy, Ferrara denied knowing Arichiello or the Zaffarones. However, he admitted to having lived his entire life in Harlem's Little Italy where they lived. The police witnesses and D.A. Swann testified that they had not threatened or been violent with Ferrara.

It took the jury only an hour and twenty minutes to find, Ferrara, age 29, guilty of first degree murder.

> "The chauffeur received the verdict quietly, but as he was led ... through the corridors of the courtroom, he came into the full gaze of his wife and his sister, Rosa, both of whom cried aloud in anguish and stretched out their arms to touch him. Both women collapsed and had to be carried out of the courthouse."[109]

A.D.A. O'Malley had urged the guilty verdict with the hope that being sentenced to the electric chair would pressure Ferrara into telling more, about the men higher up, in return for clemency.

*   *   *   *

Just as the Baff family was seeing a glimmer of justice, their competition with other poultry dealers was back in the headlines. Louis Cohen, who may have been part of the murder conspiracy, went to John J. Dillon, Commissioner of Foods and Markets, with an accusation against B. Baff & Son. They were allegedly manipulating the market and overcropping poultry, temporarily boosting its weight with a mixture of heavy food, sand and gravel. (In a separate action, Louis Cohen was preparing to sue the Baffs for slander, because they accused him of being part of the murder conspiracy. However, this case did not make it to court.).

B. Baff & Son still had about 20% of the live poultry market in New York City and branches in all boroughs. According to the New York Times of May 16,1916, the firm was owned by Harry, William and Etta Baff. Isadore was not legally an adult.

Besides, perhaps by this time, Isadore/Irving had already gone to work for his future father inlaw at Loeb & Mayer.

(Loeb & Mayer was a wholesale and retail, non-kosher meat business. It had been started by Isadore's future father-in-law, William Mayer, and by the father of Julius Loeb. Julius Loeb married William Mayer's oldest daughter, Henrietta. Isadore married Mayer's youngest daughter, Hattie. Around this time, Isadore was becoming known as Irving.)

Harry and Etta Baff went to see the Commissioner to refute Louis Cohen's charges. A former employee, now business rival, testified to their overcropping. However,

> After several poultry dealers had testified that overcropping did not prevail to any extent in the New York market, Commissioner Dillon said he would like to believe the statement, but couldn't understand why of six chickens an inspector of his department had purchased in the open market all had been overcropped, and that some of the crops weighed as much as 15 ounces.

After the hearing adjourned for the day, Etta Baff put her finger on the situation.

"This whole investigation is inspired by trade jealousy. They couldn't put us out of business by killing my father, so they are still after us. We have a big business and can undersell the others. Therefore they want Mr. Dillon to put us out of business. I will show them up if he puts me on the stand."

"I am coming here every day until it is over, and Louis Cohen had better watch out what he says about our family. There are still some of us left." [110]

Etta was described, by the Times, as the chief factor in the Baffs' business. She was involved in the business' finances, but clearly had a way with words as well as numbers. She would eventually marry, have children and be a housewife. This was usually a middle class woman's fate, even a very competent woman, in the early twentieth century.

*   *   *

In 1915, behind-the-scenes police work had lead to the convictions of Arichiello and Ferrara, in 1916. In 1916, the patient efforts of the District Attorney's office would heavily influence the action of 1917. It wasn't until nearly Christmas of 1916 that the Times revealed the return of Antonio Cardinale, sometime poultry dealer, murder plot go-between and recent soldier in the Italian Army. On December 24, 1916, they published a long article and clearly relished their story.

Despite being told by international lawyers and the U.S. State Department that it would be impossible to get Cardinale to testify in New York, the Manhattan District Attorney's Office attempted just that. During the Summer of 1916, they sent a recently hired Assistant District Attorney, William Harmon Black, to Europe which was already in the throes of World War I. He sailed to Liverpool, England, crossed to Northern Europe and traveled through Switzerland into Italy. Afterwards, he said,

> "The District Attorney had given a great deal of serious thought to the subject, because he was determined if possible to stop 'syndicate' murder in New York City."

> "District Attorney Swann discovered the whereabouts of [Antonio Cardinale] the man who had enlisted in the Italian Army, through the Italian Consul in this city ... he was the sole living person who had it in his power to bring to justice the men who were primarily responsible for one of the ugliest murders in the police annals of the city – the men who paid to have it done. The easiest way would have been to follow out the cases at hand and to have rested content with the successes already attained and closed the

case, but District Attorney Swann was determined to see the real instigators of the crime brought to justice."

In Rome, with the help of an Italian Attorney and the U.S. Ambassador to Italy, A.D.A. Black negotiated with the Italian Government. Eventually, he went to Catania, Sicily to meet with Cardinale. In his own words,

> "I appealed to Cardinale to come to America and expose the instigators of the murder and promised him full immunity from prosecution if he would do so voluntarily. He was very dubious about my authority or my good faith, and pretended to believe that if he came he might find himself prosecuted. I showed him my papers and the letter from District Attorney Swann in which he said Cardinale would not be prosecuted. I found after two or three visits that he was attempting to delay decision as long as possible, with the object of killing time. He wasn't at all inclined to return to America, because he said he wished to remain in the army. I told him that all his friends, his wife and brother and his mother wanted him to return, and he finally promised me that if his mother telegraphed him to come back he would consent to come."

Unfortunately, by this time, Cardinale's mother had passed away. Cardinale wasn't budging. Black returned to Rome and reentered negotiations with the Italian Government.

Eventually, their Appeals Court agreed to return Cardinale to the U.S. to be a witness. The Italian Government reserved the right to prosecute Cardinale; he would have immunity in the U.S. A reluctant participant, Cardinale sailed from Naples with two carbinieri, Italian cops. He arrived in New York City on November 16, 1916. He would be paid $34.50, a week, for the support of his family, while in the custody of the New York authorities.[111]

For reasons that the Times did not give, Black took a separate ship from Le Havre, France. His sailing was delayed by floating mines and a ship being blown up in the harbor. Not only did Black escape the literal mines, but the figurative ones as well. Back in 1909, New York City Police Lieutenant Joseph Petrosino had been murdered, in Palermo, Sicily, while pursuing a New York based case.

Finally, Black was home; Cardinale was back in the U.S.; Whitman had been reelected Governor and Philip Musica, con man and stool pigeon, was out of jail on a suspended sentence. The image had shifted; the prosecution of the men higher up was poised to begin.

Pursuit of the Poultry Men

In January 1917, Cardinale's testimony lead to the indictment and arrest of 6 kosher poultry men. The charge was 1st degree murder for conspiring to do away with Barnett Baff. At last it seemed, the Cohen brothers, Joseph and Jacob, and their partner and brother-in-law, David Jacobs, Abe Graff, William Simon and Moe Rosenstein were going on trial. The New York Times of January 13, 1917 described their business connections:

> Joseph and Jacob Cohen, employers of chicken "pullers," who unload crates of chickens from freight cars; Abe Graff, a member of Charles Woerner, Inc., poultry dealers [with a stand in West Washington Market]; David Jacobs, a partner in Cohen & Jacobs, poultry dealers, of 406-408 East 108th Street [East Harlem] ... William Simon, a member of the firm of Simon & Cohen, poultry dealers in East 110th Street [East Harlem], and Moe Rosenstein, known also as "Chicken Moe," a chicken puller and "strong arm" man.

Cardinale had identified Graff as the "bagman," collector of the murder fund and Joseph Cohen as assisting with the financial aspect of the conspiracy. The six Jewish prisoners pleaded not guilty.[112]

By this time, it had become clearer why Cardinale was testifying. It wasn't merely that A.D.A. Black prevailed upon the Italian Government. Cardinale found his own agenda: "It was only when names of many of his close friends were mentioned as suspects that he was induced to name the men who he said really were the principals."[113] The Jewish and Italian conspirators had parted ways.

*   *   *

Meanwhile, out in the market place, prices were rising. Increased urbanization and the approach of the country's entry into World War I were at least partly to blame. In February, there were food riots and a consumer boycott was started against onions, potatoes and poultry. By late March, most wholesalers and retailers had bowed to the boycott and weren't selling the "prohibited" commodities, but not Harry Baff. As a receiver of shipments, wholesaler and retailer, like Barnett, Harry did not feel the pressure to join the boycott. As the only buyer in the market, he could have a low wholesale cost and pass the low price on to the customers in his shops and those of his associates.

Boycotters threatened his retail stores, but Harry raked in his profits. His retail competitors could not afford his wholesale prices and still sell at a price that would attract customers. It was like Barnett versus everyone all over again.[114]

*   *   *   *

Back on the crime beat, a date was set for Ferrara's execution at Sing Sing prison. He was slated to go to the electric chair during the week of April 16, 1917.[115] The United States had by this time declared war on Germany and begun to send troops to Europe.

The prosecution of the Jewish conspirators was going less well. They did not have a trial date prior to the Fall. Therefore their attorney asked that they be released on bail. District Attorney Swann consented. The reason he gave was that Cardinale was critically ill. Clearly he couldn't ask to move up the case on the court calendar and without Cardinale he might not have a case. Five of the prisoners were freed on $25,000 bail each. (William Simon was prosecuted later than the others and may have been released much earlier.).[116]

Musical Chairs

Again, the Baff Murder Case slipped out of the headlines, but there was a great deal going on behind the scenes. For one thing, there had been a game of legal musical chairs. Walter R. Deuel, the Assistant District Attorney (A.D.A) originally assigned to prosecute Barnett's murderers, had become the private attorney for Arichiello and Ferrara.

Con man, Phillip Musica, was out on parole and supposedly reformed. It was probably his role as Manhattan D.A. Charles Whitman's pet stool pigeon that lead to his hiring by Whitman's gubernatorial administration. Calling himself William Johnson, he became an investigator in the New York State Attorney General's Office. As later events would prove, he would never stop being a consummate con artist. He also had ties to New York City's Italian immigrant community.

Cardinale's illness may have been a stalling tactic. He had already decided to testify in a way that would hurt the men higher up, but with an eye to advancing the cause of his fellow Italians. Arichiello was rumored to have wealthy connections in the "Lupo gang" who spent a great deal on his defense.[117]   Cardinale, Musica or both could happily have been paid to influence the outcome of the murder case in favor of the Italian gangsters.

Deuel and Musica used their connections to Governor Charles Whitman to bring about the next development. Whitman's tendency to step into the limelight could have been a factor too. His law and order stance in the Rosenthal Case had brought him to the Governor's Mansion. If he hoped to get to the White House, as some other of New York's Governors had, a win in the Baff Case would help. Besides if someone was to get the glory, why not the State Republican Administration instead of the City's Tammany Hall Democratic D.A. Swann. Sometime in April or May 1917, Whitman took the Barnett Baff Case from the District Attorney's Office and gave it to the New York State Attorney General's Office. His given reason was that the prosecution of the case was being delayed. Should he have said this after the patient and impressive work of the New York City Police and of A.D.A. Black?

The immediate beneficiary of these machinations was Ferrara. His execution had to be postponed, because the State wanted his testimony. Philip Musica, styled as investigator William Johnson, was assigned to gathering evidence in the Baff Murder case. He went into Sing Sing prison saying, untruthfully, that he was a Deputy Attorney General.[118]

The kaleidoscope had been shaken and a new pattern had appeared. The Baff case was being commandeered by men with agendas other than justice.

Escaped

More than two years after the murder, police were still pounding the pavement, rounding up suspects. Though it proved to be a red herring, they succeeded in finding two of their quarry in Los Angeles.

> Trapped in a car, where he was working as a cleaner, Jack Rizotta ... was arrested here tonight ... His brother Ben, wanted on the same charge, ran when he saw the officers and escaped. Many shots were exchanged between the escaping man and the police.[119]

The next day a less violent, but potentially more important escape occurred. Police informant and material witness Carmine Di Paolo, of the early attempts to murder Barnett, escaped from the 12th Floor of the House of Detention at 49 Lafayette Street,* in lower Manhattan. It was not an escape worthy of his contemporary Houdini. It was more a case of official carelessness, with or without a monetary motivation.

> According to Keepers Dorcey and Grier, the fugitive received permission to wash his

---

* This was a holding facility for witnesses, not the Tombs.

hands, and when he did not return they found he had vanished.

An investigation disclosed that Di Paolo had pried the grating loose from the washroom window and made his way to freedom by way of the fire escape. He used a painter's ladder in climbing over the fence in the yard.[120]

Di Paolo had been held for about 15 months.

Prosecution of the Poultrymen

By mid-June 1917, the Attorney General's office, in haste, had already convened an extraordinary grand jury. Deputy Attorneys General Alfred Becker and James O'Malley were on the case. At the start of the proceedings, Justice Arthur S. Tompkins told the jury, "It is your sworn duty to file indictments against those accused, no matter how high their position or their standing in the community, provided the evidence justifies such indictments."[121]

Before June was out, four men were indicted and on trial: Brothers Joseph and Jacob Cohen, David Jacobs and Abraham (Abe) Graff. Moses ("Chicken Moe") Rosenstein had cut a deal. He would be allowed to plead guilty to manslaughter in return for being a witness for the State. Ferrara and Arichiello would also be testifying against the Jewish poultrymen.

The jurors were vetted, by the defense, for being overly influenced by someone in power pressing for conviction. (Most likely the prosecution planned to invoke Governor Whitman's interest in punishing the men higher up.). The prosecution asked prospective jurors if they were against capital punishment and if they would respect testimony by accomplices who were testifying for the State. Of course, only men were impaneled for the jury.[122] Women were still second class citizens who didn't have the vote.

On the first day of the trial, Antonio Cardinale testified to the business rivalries involving Barnett Baff and the defendants. "Joseph Cohen said Baff was the worst crook in the business. He said it was impossible to exist with him."[123] Cardinale talked about the early history of intimidation leading up to the murder. He mentioned gangster Joe Sarro or Sorro, of the failed Arverne bombing, in connection with this phase of operations.

Deputy A.G. O'Malley attempted to garner sympathy for Moe Rosenstein saying that other conspirators had considered killing him, because they distrusted him. In fact, Rosenstein did leave town supposedly in fear for his life. He was arrested in Chicago.[124] Then he had decided to testify for the state and squander any trust which the other poultrymen might have placed in him.

On the second day of Cardinale's testimony, he was cooperative until he was asked a question about the Sicilian Gangsters. Then he shut down.

> Cardinale: "I refuse to answer that question."
>
> Judge Tompkins: "Are you afraid to answer?"
>
> Cardinale: "No, but I won't answer that question."
>
> Judge Tompkins: "What is your reason for not answering?"
>
> Cardinale: "If I told you my reason, I would be telling everything."[125]

Cardinale said that he was testifying against the Cohens to put blame where it belonged.

> "I couldn't keep it on my conscience," he said. Then when he was asked if he couldn't make his conscience let him reveal the names of the two men who did the shooting, he said his conscience told him not to do that because he had gotten the two [gunmen] into enough trouble by hiring them to kill Baff.[126]

Cardinale was neither about to implicate his fellow Sicilians nor do more than hint at the conspiracy to both implicate the poultrymen and exonerate Arichiello and the other gangsters.

In other testimony, a 1913 meeting of the Live Poultry Dealers Protective Association was described by Elias B. Goodman, an attorney, who had been in attendance:

> Seventy to eighty poultry dealers were present ... among them Joseph Cohen and his partner, William Simon. Simon ... made a speech in which he attacked Baff and accused him of overcropping his poultry and ruining the business for the rest of the dealers. ... a woman dealer, Mrs. Pishkosh, shouted that Baff "ought to be drowned." ... Simon himself ... entered into such a tirade against Baff that ... Goodman had to call him to order and remind him that as Chairman of the meeting Simon ought to refrain from such "wild statements".[127]

The attempt to exonerate Arichiello continued with the testimony of Ferrara, the driver of the getaway car.

> Ferrara declared that all the testimony that he gave implicating Arichiello and Reno [Rina] was perjured and manufactured under duress and compulsion to suit the theories of the detectives working on the case ... he insisted that Arichiello and Reno were not in the murder party and that the real gunmen were Charles Dragnia ... and "Tita"...

> Both Dragnia and Tita were in the Tombs on a blackmailing charge when Ferrara was arrested in February 1916, in connection

with the Baff murder. Ferrara did not say a word at the time of their alleged complicity in the crime under the grueling examination of the police and District Attorney's Office . . .

About a month ago, after Ferrara had made several attempts through his attorneys to get a new trial, he decided ... to disclose the names of the real gunmen ... Dragnia and Tita were traced to San Francisco. Dragnia was arrested, but Tita escaped by a hair's breadth. He was actually in the hands of a detective, when he suddenly slipped off his coat, dashed into a side street, followed by a fusillade of shots, and disappeared. He is still at large.

Ferrara quite vividly painted an alternate reality.

"It was early in November 1914, when Charlie Dragnia came to me in Little Italy and said, 'I want a poultry dealer downtown killed. There's $300 in it, and a closed car must be used.' He introduced me to Tita, and we drove downtown to look over the ground. I had a chauffeur with me named Dopey John, and I told Charlie that I intended to use him when the trick was pulled. But Charlie said, 'Don't do that. We have you on the job, and we don't want it advertised all over Harlem.' He told me to get the fastest car I could."

"I worked in Patsy Garafola's garage, so on November 24, the day of the shooting, I told my boss that I had a hospital call for that afternoon. I took the biggest and speediest car we had, and met Charlie and Tita at 103d Street and First Avenue. They had a rifle with a Maxim silencer, which they put together. We went down to West Washington Market, stopping at Fifteenth Street and Tenth Avenue. There they got out and walked west on Fourteenth Street. After they were gone twenty minutes they came back and ordered me to drive into the market."

"We went into the market, but there were a lot of people there, and a man on horseback. I said, 'There are too many people around; wait till dark, and I'll take a chance.' He said, 'All right,' and he and Tita went away for about an hour. Dragnia came back about 6 o'clock and said, "Drive in now. There are not many people about.' I drove into the market and was ordered to stop at Gansevoort Street and Thirteenth Avenue, on the northeast. He told me to back up, and I took a diagonal position facing southeast. I was smoking a cigarette at the wheel, and an officer passed swinging his club. Dragnia, after he left me, went on Thirteenth Avenue."

" I stayed on the corner for ten minutes and heard two shots from the north. I tried to look around to see what happened, and I saw Tita and Dragnia running toward the car. Dragnia had told me to keep the motor running when he left. Tita got in and Dragnia hopped on the running board. I heard people shouting, 'Stop them! Stop them!' But I put on speed and hurried south on West Street just missing an auto truck and a team. Then I drove to 104th Street and First Avenue. I got $12 for the use of the car."

Ferrara continued to embellish with details about the conversation in the car and being paid off by Dragnia. He claimed that he had been forced to lie, because of brutal treatment at the hands of the police; "I was afraid, I was afraid, I tell you, of the detectives. I had to tell the same story that they wanted me to tell. They wouldn't have anything else."[128]

Ferrara also claimed that Ippolito Greco and Antonio Zaffarone had nothing to do with the murder. Based on bartender Luporte's testimony and that of others, Greco was clearly involved. Zaffarone had confessed his involvement in one of the murder attempts. Besides, Ferrara was the first man arrested in the case. It is unlikely that the police would have wanted him to agree to a particular story. They didn't have someone else's evidence that needed corroborating and the D.A.'s office had also been in on the questioning. Clearly Ferrara was a desperate liar. After he was already in jail, Ferrara had said that he was out of work, not working at the garage. Additionally, his new story had a gun with a silencer which nonetheless produced audible shots.

Since Ferrara was in Sing Sing and Philip Musica, a.k.a. William Johnson, was there "investigating" an arrangement could have been reached to whitewash Arichiello. Even if no one believed Ferrara's new story, it would have shed doubt on Ferrara's veracity. Since Ferrara was already condemned to death, perjuring himself would not have increased his risk, but it might have given his fellow gangsters better incentive to take care of Ferrara's wife and two children.

The next day of the trial was an emotional one for Ferrara. He stuck by his new testimony about police coercion. The excitement came during the lunchtime recess when he was permitted to walk around in the courthouse, for exercise, with two keepers. His wife, Mamie, who had been hysterical at the end of his trial, made another scene. She "eluded his keepers, and rushing up to him, threw her arms around him and kissed him. The couple were separated and Mrs. Ferrara became hysterical."[129]

The next witness was a one time employee of Cardinale's, Joseph Sorro, one of the Arverne bombers. He told of that job being done at the

behest of Joe Cohen. He implicated brothers Joe
and Jacob Cohen and brother-in-law David Jacobs
in torching the market of Aaron Newmark, a Baff
ally. Sorro related that after the fire, Cardinale said
that Joseph Cohen wanted Barnett Baff murdered.

> "I'm up against it, but I'll see Greco, and he'll
> fix me up all right," Sorro quoted Cardinale
> as saying to him.

> The witness said that a few days later he met
> Greco, the Cohen brothers, Jacobs and
> Cardinale, who, he said, were at the time
> discussing with Greco the terms for
> committing the murder.

> "Tony Cardinale told Greco that Joe Cohen
> wanted to pay him $500. Greco laughed and
> said that such a sum wouldn't buy his men
> cigars. I don't know how much Greco asked."

> "Did you hear what the $500 was for?" Mr.
> Becker [Deputy A.G.] asked.

> " Yes, it was to kill Baff. Cardinale told me
> so," Sorro replied.[130]

Sorro's testimony was especially important. He was
clearly a criminal, but he did not play a role in
Barnett's murder. Therefore, unlike Ferrara and
Cardinale, he was a non-accomplice witness.
Having such a witness was nearly essential to
making the case against the poultrymen. (It had
been the belated finding of such a witness that had

made the corrupt cop Charles Becker's conviction "stick" when the Rosenthal murder case was tried for the second time.).

A.T. Pearson, Barnett's old business ally, testified, "On one occasion I heard Joe Cohen say that Baff would get his some day, and that he was surprised something hadn't happened before. I heard dozens of others speak in the same tone about Baff." [131]   Another witness, Daniel Jones, a chicken handler, saw one of the earlier murder attempts in which Abe Graff set a man in a loft with a gun. He claimed that Cardinale and "Tita" were in the loft too.

Garage owner Patrick Garafola identified the getaway car. However, he backed Ferrara's earlier story about borrowing the car to visit someone in the hospital.[132] Again, there was cooperation with the authorities up to a point, but a closing of ranks among the Italians to protect each other.

The next day, "Chicken Moe" Rosenstein testified against the Cohens and Graff who had all pulled him into the murder conspiracy.   He admitted tipping his hat to signal the gunmen when he met Barnett.   He also admitted to being a chicken thief. He had helped the conspirators, but now he had turned state's evidence to save his neck. The defense attorney, Frank Moss, suggested that Moe had been offered a bribe, by Harry Baff, for his incriminating testimony about Barnett's enemies. Chicken Moe's reply, "No such luck."[133] Rosenstein's only known loyalty was to himself.

Joseph Cohen took the stand in his own defense. He would claim from first to last that he was being framed. This time was the first. He disclaimed ever discussing the Arverne bombing with Cardinale. He said that he was approached by Joseph Sorro who said he had been arrested for planting a bomb.

> "What bomb is this and why do you tell this to me?" Cohen said he asked.

> "Why the one you paid me $100 for when you promised to give me $300," the witness quoted Sorro as saying.

> "Then I said to him," Cohen continued, "What is this frame-up you're starting? Just step out where everyone can hear you talk."

> Cohen said that his relations with Barnet [sic] Baff had always been friendly. As proof of this he mentioned several occasions when he and the poultry dealer had dined together. The witness had said that the

death of Baff had caused much trouble in a financial way.[134]

Joseph Cohen was clearly lying. If he and Barnett had been friends, Harry Baff would not have accused him of being a murderer. Harry, as Barnett's son and sole partner, would have known if Cohen had been his father's friend. Eventually, too, Cohen admitted that he hadn't been to Barnett's funeral as a good friend would have.

He also seemed to be lying about his involvement with the Live Poultry Dealers' Association. He was their Treasurer and yet he claimed,

> "I was only a figurehead in the association. I don't know what went on there or how the money was expended. No one asked me for an accounting and I never handled any cash."

> ... He reiterated that he had always been friendly to [Barnett] Baff and to Harry Baff ...

> "Didn't you know that Harry Baff had made a speech in Chicago, in which he said that you were worse than the Czar of Russia in the unloading business?" Mr. O'Malley asked.

> "I don't remember," Cohen replied.[135]

Not surprisingly, Joseph Cohen was convicted of first degree murder and sentenced to the electric chair. He received the verdict calmly. By comparison, Abraham Graff "was found guilty of manslaughter in the first degree and was sentenced to a term in Sing Sing" of ten to twenty years. Graff threw himself on the mercy of the court, saying,

> "Since I was 12 years old, I have supported myself. I have never taken a dishonest penny. I had no part in the crime for which I was convicted, and I ask the mercy of the court for my wife and two children, who are absolutely dependent on me for support."

> To this plea Judge Tompkins replied:

> "The innocent are always the ones who are made to suffer most. But in convicting you for manslaughter the jury displayed great mercy. In your case, Mr. Graff, the jury could just as easily have brought in a verdict of murder in the first degree as manslaughter, and you have been very fortunate to escape."[136]

Of course, Joseph Cohen's relatives, Jacob Cohen and David Jacobs, were even luckier. They were acquitted.

Joseph Cohen and Abe Graff, left the Tombs for Sing Sing prison. They traveled up the Hudson River to Ossining, New York* in the company of two sheriffs. Cohen expressed confidence that he would be freed on appeal. On the trip from the Ossining train station to the prison, he persuaded the sheriffs to let him stop for a steak dinner.

Based on Cardinale's testimony, Arichiello's attorney, Walter Deuel, asked Judge Tompkins to have Arichiello retried. New York State, in the person of Deputy A.G. O'Malley, did not object.[137] Arichiello had been fortunate in having the A.G.'s office prosecuting the murder case. The machinations of Cardinale, Deuel and Philip Musica were starting to work.

Meanwhile, in a separate case, Antonio Zaffarone had been sentenced to five to fifteen years in Sing Sing for complicity in Barnett's murder.

> The Court took into consideration the fact that Zaffarone had been of material aid to the State in the search for the Baff murderers. Zaffarone admitted his part in

---

* The location of Sing Sing, up the Hudson River from New York City, is the origin of the use of "being sent up the river" to denote conviction and imprisonment.

the plot and first told the authorities that Baff was murdered at the instigation of business rivals.[138]

Next up for indictment and arrest was William Simon. Besides making "wild statements" against Barnett, he stood accused of collecting the funds used to pay for the murder. By then it was mid-September 1917.

Any sense of vindication that the Baff family might have felt was short lived. In October Judge Tompkins ordered a new trial for Arichiello. Then in February 1918, B. Baff & Son as well as related businesses were shut down by the United States Food Administration. This time the trouble did not seem to come from commercial rivals, but from the business practices of the Baffs themselves.

With the nation fighting in World War I, New York City suffered food shortages. Unscrupulous wholesalers took advantage of the situation. The Baffs were engaged in price gouging and this *did* have to do with the price of eggs. The Baffs, or at least Harry, controlled four firms: B. Baff & Son, Baff & Son, Fannie Baff and Harry & Fannie Baff. The scam went like this: one of the four companies would buy

Eggs for 37½ cents a dozen. It, in turn, sold to one of the other firms mentioned for 48½ cents. When the eggs finally left the Baff circle . . . They brought 51½ cents a dozen, or a profit of 14 cents.[139]

Harry lost his license to deal in eggs and poultry, a suspension that continued for months.[140]

While the livelihood of the Baffs was being constrained, the life of Joseph Cohen got no more than a temporary reprieve. On May 28, 1918, the New York State Court of Appeals confirmed Cohen's conviction and death sentence. On June 27th, the Grand Jury that indicted Cohen for murder was reconvened. They were to hear that Cohen's friends tried to bribe Cardinale to change his testimony. A bribe of $5,000 was offered to Cardinale's wife if she could persuade him to change his testimony implicating Cohen. Less than a week later, Cohen was faring a little better: He would get a stay of execution until after co-conspirator William Simon's trial.

Frank Moss, attorney for Cohen, and a committee headed by Dr. Samuel Buchler[*],

---

[*] On the face of things, Joseph Cohen's cause could only be enhanced by the support of a chaplain and rabbi. However, Buchler was also an attorney. He was disbarred, in 1932,

formerly chaplain at Sing Sing Prison and now Deputy Commissioner of Charities of New York, requested a postponement of the execution on the ground that evidence will be offered at the Simon Trial to prove that Cohen was the victim of a conspiracy.[141]

No effort was spared in keeping Joseph Cohen alive. Subsequently, the U.S. Supreme Court refused to hear Cohen's case and a State commission refused to judge him insane.

For the next four months of 1918, the murder trials were out of the headlines. World War I ended on November 11th. The fourth anniversary of the murder came and went. Finally, on December 3rd, the New York Times reported:

New evidence that is believed to be strong enough to reach the entire conspiracy involved in the murder of Barnet Baff ... has been obtained by Deputy State Attorney General Becker and Special Deputy O'Malley. A special Grand Jury is to be impaneled to hear this evidence, and the State will ask for at least twenty-five indictments against men alleged to have contributed to the murder fund and those implicated in hiring the

---

and convicted of fraudulent activity and, after serving his sentence, was indicted for subsequent activities. His support of Joseph Cohen was a criminal advocating for another criminal.

gunmen, some of whom were believed to be business rivals of Baff.

In this new investigation the reason for the secret release from the Tombs Prison of William Simon on Tuesday was disclosed yesterday. It was said he had agreed to turn State's evidence and to tell what he knows of the murder conspiracy and the part each individual had in carrying out the plan.

Mr. Becker believes this new evidence will clear up the case.[142]

Here then was the high water mark of justice: Joseph Cohen and Frank Ferrara were on death row awaiting execution. Abraham Graff, Moses ("Chicken Moe") Rosenstein, Antonio Zaffarone and Giuseppe Arichiello were in prison.

The Beginning of The End

Nine days later, the work of the police, courts, District Attorney and Attorney General, which looked substantial, began to fall into fragments. The first development seemed like a swap of two steps backwards for twenty-five steps forwards, but it turned out to be giving up two birds in the hand for twenty-five in the bush. In the interest of pursuing the twenty-five or so poultrymen who hired the gunmen, two men, who had already been convicted of participation in the murder of Barnett, received suspended sentences. Instead of going to the electric chair or serving out a prison term, Giuseppe Arichiello and Moe Rosenstein were to join William Simon in testifying for the State. These three witnesses were in protective custody.

Governor Whitman, now a lame duck, had stuck his oar in one last time by authorizing an extraordinary trial term. Justice Arthur S. Tompkins, of the original trial of the "men higher up," presided again saying, "The important thing is to convict the men who hired the gunmen that did the shooting." The Attorney General's Office had men being watched; arrests were imminent.[143]

On January 1, 1919, Democrat Alfred Smith started his first term as New York State Governor. Before he had a chance to get involved in the Baff case, the Federal Government unexpectedly intervened in the person of Missouri's Senator James A. Reed.

Senator Reed Inquires

Though a Democrat, Senator Reed opposed his own party's president, Woodrow Wilson, on joining the League of Nations. He was also an outspoken critic of the subsequent Republican Presidents. Most important to the Baff case, Reed was an anti-corruption crusader. He held hearings and he rooted out the influence of lobbyists and campaign contributors.

With World War I over for about two months, Senator Reed was investigating whether or not newspaper publisher William Randolph Hearst[*] had been unjustly accused of pro-German activities. The New York State Attorney General's office had been involved in keeping an eye on German sympathizers. As a consequence, Reed spent a long time questioning Deputy Attorney General Alfred Becker (who had prosecuted the men higher up) about his use of investigator Philip Musica, a.k.a. William Johnson.

---

[*] Hearst was represented at the hearing by, among others, former Assistant District Attorney William DeFord of the Poultry Trust Prosecution.

The Senator succeeded in getting into the record that Philip M. Musica, who is employed by the Attorney General of New York as an investigator, pleaded guilty to grand larceny several years ago and was liberated under a suspended sentence. Mr. Becker countered by proving that before entering the employ of the State Mr. Musica was employed by District Attorneys Whitman, James A. Perkins, and Edward Swann, and that he entered the State's service as the result of a recommendation from Mr. Swann's Office.

"I have watched the conduct of Musica since he came to my office," said Mr. Becker, "and as a result of my acquaintance with him I have been convinced that there is such a thing as reform. I know his past, and I know how hard he has worked to make good, and I stand by him. I am his friend, and I shall continue to be."[144]

Events were to prove that Mr. Becker was yet another victim of a Philip Musica con job. Convincing the authorities that he had gone straight, while secretly working for a gangster like Arichiello, must have been one of the great thrills of Musica's life though definitely not the last one.

Senator Reed also tied Musica to the Baff case:

"Was it not the theory of this man Musica ...that it was not the defendant[s] Archiello [and] Ferrari [sic], who had confessed, but a man named Joseph Cohen that was the real murderer and Cohen was convicted and is now under sentence of death...?"

"The theory that Cohen was the man was proved. Ferrari [sic] still stands convicted as one of the murderers, and Archiello was given a new trial," replied Mr. Becker.

Senator Reed entered upon a long series of questions about the Baff case, and finally said:

"So the interesting situation develops that Musica was the desk mate of Duel [sic]. Duel was the attorney for the convicted murderer. Musica was in close touch with Cardinale, the witness who was to put the blame on Cohen. Duel went to Governor Whitman and proceeded in getting the case transferred to you, and you and Musica succeeded in getting Cohen convicted and Mr. Duel's client went scot free."

"That is about 50 per cent right," replied Mr. Becker.[145]

After this hearing, the pursuit of twenty-five poultry men was swept from the headlines. The conduct of the case against Joseph Cohen became the focus of events.

Perjury

Based on an appeal from Senator Reed and the advice of New York's Attorney General, Governor Smith gave Cohen and Ferrara a three month reprieve from the electric chair. Early in 1919,[146] District Attorney Swann started investigating the conduct of the case against Cohen, particularly the role of Joseph Sorro. This would prove to be a shifting picture:

> Joseph Sarro [sic], who was expected to be the chief witness in Swann's investigation, recanted and told Becker he had falsely accused himself of perjury because his life had been threatened.[147]

Cardinale was also called to testify. While he was as ready as ever to implicate Joseph Cohen in the plot to kill Barnett, he was otherwise not very helpful about answering Assistant District Attorney Ferdinand Pecora's questions. Given the terms of his loan to the case, by the Italian Government, the Court could do little to compel his cooperation.[148]

As the perjury investigation continued and led to Sorro's endictment, Governor Smith extended Cohen's and Ferrara's reprieves. It was the third stay of execution for Cohen, the sixth for Ferrara.[149]

Meanwhile, on August 20, 1919, the New York Times offered this summation of Cardinale's role in the case:

> A self-confessed murder accomplice, Antonio Cardinale, who testified in the Criminal Branch of the Supreme Court that he had hired the gunmen who murdered Barnet Baff ... after which he fled to Italy, and was returned by the Italian Government on the agreement by the Department of State that he would not be prosecuted, but used as a witness only, was freed yesterday from the law's restraint, and he will be paid $1,500 as compensation for the time he was detained here. Cardinale had previously, at different times, been paid $1,500 toward the support of his wife, and in return for this cost to the county he has given practically no assistance in the prosecution of the Baff conspirators, because he refused to identify or to mention the names of the men who fired the shots at Baff.
>
> This situation is not due to any fault of the American law officers nor of the State Department, but to the rigidness of the Italian law which bars extradition action for trial of its citizens in a foreign country. According to the terms of the agreement by which Cardinale was sent here by the Italian authorities, he was "loaned" as a witness, but the intimation then was that he would be tried when returned to Italy for his offense here, the evidence and testimony against him to be sent to Italy for that purpose. Attorneys familiar with the Baff case expressed the opinion yesterday that it was unlikely that he would be prosecuted

there, it having been reported that the statute of limitations would free him when he reaches Italy.

... Cardinale was not imprisoned here. That he should be free in his movements was insisted upon by the Italian authorities. He had a guard, but when out of court he could go and come as he pleased with this police guard, and room and board, in addition to his compensation, were provided for him.

However, had he wanted it, he would have had to provide his own needlework pillow saying "Crime *Does* Pay."

Cardinale returned to Italy and the legal aftermath of the Baff murder ground on. Cohen and Ferrara applied for another stay of execution which they received. Cohen had been on death row for over two years, Ferrara for even longer.[150]

Those familiar with Sing Sing prison provided evidence in the perjury inquiry being directed by Judge John F. McIntyre[*]:

Dr. Samuel Buchler, Jewish Chaplain at Sing Sing Prison, said he had seen Jacob Lubin

---

[*] Before he became a judge, McIntyre was the defense attorney in the first trial of Charles Becker, the accused murderer of Herman Rosenthal. Thanks to Musica, Judge McIntyre could side with the defendents in the Baff Case.

talking to certain notorious gangsters at the prison, who, he was told, had been involved in the Baff case.

Lubin, who was employed as an investigator [stool pigeon[151]] in the case, was questioned. He said:

"I don't know whether Cohen is guilty or not, but I do know that the evidence that convicted him was perjured evidence, procured by Philip Musica, working for an attorney. This attorney introduced me to Musica, who posed as one Johnson and claimed he was a Deputy Attorney General. I went to Sing Sing with Musica to get witnesses who would swear to certain things. Musica said he was not interested in Cohen, but wanted to free Arichello and Ferrara."[152]

The eventual outcome of the inquiry was that Judge McIntyre wrote to Governor Smith urging commutation of Joseph Cohen's sentence. The essence of his written argument was:

"At the trial of Cohen the principal witness called against him was Antonio Cardinale, who was himself ... charged with the murder of Baff ... Cardinale by his testimony in the Cohen case was clearly an accomplice in the murder of Baff, hence his testimony requires corroboration before any conviction could be had.

"The principal corroborating witness ... was ... [Joseph] Sorro, whose testimony was of a very damaging nature. It is extremely doubtful in my opinion if a conviction could have been obtained against Joseph Cohen without the testimony of Sorro. In his seventy-five page deposition [in the perjury inquiry] ... he retracted practically every item of testimony given by him upon the trial of Joseph Cohen. He declared that all such testimony was false, and that he had been suborned to give such testimony by one Philip M. Musica ... [Sorro and Cardinale] declined to answer most of the questions addressed to them by both the District Attorney and myself ... the very shifty and evasive attitude adopted by these two witnesses in the light of the very detailed retraction Sorro had previously made on oath, are among the principal elements of the conclusion that the sentence of death should be commuted."[153]

However, Judge Tompkins, who presided at Cohen's original trial, opposed commuting his sentence to life in prison, saying, "I haven't any doubt of the guilt of the defendant".[154]

After receiving the advice of both judges and conferring with Deputy A.G. Becker, Governor Smith took a middle course postponing execution, but not commuting the death sentence of Cohen or Ferrara. This eleventh hour reprieve received its due drama in the New York Times of December 11, 1919:

The stay was the twelfth time that Ferrera has gone to the very steps of the chair and has been saved. Tonight's stay to Ferrera established a state record of reprieves. The young, frailly built Italian has sat through three years of waiting in the death house at Sing Sing, and this evening when a keeper carried the news to him he found him sitting on the edge of his bed. Hope was gone this time, for, with the passage of seconds, dawn, the time of death, was speeding on. Yet when the keeper told him the news he failed to display much emotion.

"I am glad to get anything, Joe," he said dully, "maybe I can get to sleep now."

As for Cohen, it was the fifth time that executive clemency has saved him in the two and a half years of his life in the death house.

"That is good news," he said when the keeper passing down the corridor delivered his second message.

Harry Again

As the perjury inquiry was beginning to unravel the murder case, the business that made and (indirectly) broke Barnett was also unraveling. Harry, about half a generation older than his siblings, was probably responsible. (By this time, Irving was married and working for his father-in-law.)

On October 8, 1919, B. Baff and Sons filed for involuntary bankruptcy. On October 10, 1919, a small article appeared in the New York Times under the headline "Receiver for Baff's Business." It read, in its entirety:

> Supreme Court Justice Gavegan yesterday appointed John C. Hertle receiver of the poultry business of Harry Baff, Inc., in West Washington Market, in a suit by Barnet Cohen, stockholder and large creditor, against Harry, Rose and Fannie Baff, directors and stockholders. The plaintiff alleged that Harry Baff, son of Barnet [sic] Baff, who was murdered in the market several years ago, mismanaged the business. The defendant denied the allegations.

Rose Baff was Harry's wife, Fannie, his mother. It was an era when one's reputation was often the reputation of one's family. Harry would forever be known as Barnett's son. Now he was the son who had lost the business over which his father had given his life. About a month later, he was accused of violating bankruptcy law. He was held on $10,000 bail for making "A false oath and account, as to material facts in the bankruptcy proceedings."[155] However, as subsequent events proved, Harry managed to struggle along in the meat and poultry business.

Executive Clemency

Finally, in February 1920, Governor Smith decided to commute the sentences of Joseph Cohen and Frank Ferrara to life in prison. He was not doubting their guilt, but felt that justice would still be served without the death penalty. He also cited Judge McIntyre's recommendation regarding Cohen, from the perjury hearing, and the fact that the Court of Appeals had been less than unanimous in confirming Cohen's conviction. Ferrara received his commutation on the recommendation of Attorney General Newton who said that he had been helpful to the State of New York. The treatment of Cohen and Ferrara fit a pattern of Governor Smith extending executive clemency.[156]

Ferrara had been in the death house, at Sing Sing, for three and a half years, a record length of time, and had his execution stayed thirteen times. Cohen had "only" been there two and a half years. The next stop for both was the prison hospital. Each had succumbed to the post-World War I flu epidemic. Cohen was also suffering a nervous breakdown.[157]

The year 1920 also saw the publication of *Hey Rub-a-Dub-Dub: A Book of the Mystery and Wonder and Terror of Life*. It was a book of non-fiction by the socialist author Theodore Dreiser who was better known for his novels. In a litany of criticism of the American national character, the murder of Barnett is one of Dreiser's cases in point:

> One Barnet Baff, wholesale chicken merchant in New York City, was murdered because he would not enter upon a scheme with other chicken-wholesalers to fix prices and extort a higher profit from the public. Secondary executors, but not primary instigators or murderers, were caught and electrocuted.[158]

While this is a poor description of the reasons for the murder and an incorrect description of the results, it is a good reflection of the nastiness, greed and injustice of the murder.

Trying the Lawyer

February 1920 found Judge Mulqueen presiding over yet another Baff Case Grand Jury. Joseph Sorro, former Governor Whitman and attorney Walter Deuel were all targets. Not surprisingly, Joseph Sorro was indicted for perjury committed as a witness in Joseph Cohen's trial.

Given Senator Reed's investigation, it was also logical that the Grand Jury wanted Attorney Walter Deuel to be investigated by the Bar Association. They pointed out that

> "Deuel acted as attorney or counsel for various persons indicted for the Baff murder, despite the fact that prior thereto he had for many months conducted an official investigation as a Deputy Assistant District Attorney of New York County into the facts and circumstances surrounding the murder."[159]

Just as Charles Whitman would be criticized fifty years later for his conduct of the Charles Becker/Herman Rosenthal Case, the Grand Jury was critical, in 1920, of his role in the Baff case. They did not approve of his taking the case away from District Attorney Swann. They recognized this as being done for the benefit of Attorney Deuel who was defending Arichiello and Ferrara. Governor

Whitman was seen, by the Grand Jury, to have taken sides in the Baff Case and, on his watch, the case had been tainted by perjury.

Eventually, the Grand Jury indicted Deuel and Philip Musica for attempted subornation of perjury. Specifically

> Having induced Hyman Berger and George Davis, convicts at Sing Sing, to stand ready to testify falsely against several other convicts, who were reported to be about to give evidence for Joseph Cohen.[160]

The next day

> Mr. Deuel walked into the court room unaccompanied and asked Judge Mulqueen, before whom he had appeared many times as a prosecutor, if the report of his indictment were true. Judge Mulqueen said the indictment had been returned and, with the assent of an Assistant District Attorney, fixed the bail at $5,000. Mr. Deuel's plea: not guilty.[161]

Joseph Cohen Again and Again

Finally in 1921, the perjury case against Joseph Sorro got underway. Another Joseph, Joseph Cohen, was wanted as a witness. It would be the first time that he would be out of Sing Sing since he was originally condemned to the electric chair. However, it took prison officials a while to figure out for whom they had received a writ of habeas corpus. It wasn't until they had questioned three of their five Joseph Cohens that they knew they had the right one.[162]

Shortly after, Joseph Cohen's Attorney, John J. Goldstein, filed a motion asking that Cohen receive a new trial. Joseph Sorro's perjured testimony was the basis of the request. Sorro's role as a non-accomplice witness had been key to Cohen's conviction. By 1921, Sorro was claiming that he had testified falsely. The New York Times reported this latest development on January 30, 1921* and described the Baff case as "one of the most complicated criminal cases or series of cases

---

* This was eleven days after the birth of Barnett's fourth grandchild, Beverly Baff.

on record in New York". And there was more to come.

Less than two months later, the Court was reserving judgment on a new trial for Joseph Cohen. They were awaiting the outcome of Sorro's upcoming trial for perjury. While Sorro had confessed to commiting perjury, he had since recanted his confession,[163] an extremely muddy situation.

A.G. Becker in Hot Water Again

Since Barnett's murder, Charles S. Whitman had assumed the Governorship of New York State. After serving two terms, he had been unseated by Democrat Alfred E. Smith. Smith had been replaced, after one term, by Republican Nathan Miller who took office January 1, 1921. By this time, Alfred Becker was no longer Deputy Attorney General. However, he turned up in the Baff case, again, as defense lawyer for accused perjurer, Joseph Sorro. This lead to Assistant District Attorney Ferdinand Pecora criticizing Becker's professional conduct and filing a grievance with the New York State Bar Association.

The essence of Pecora's charge was that Becker, as Attorney General, had obtained information about the State's case against Sorro. This information was provided on a strictly confidential basis, but then Becker became counsel for Sorro effectively using information provided in confidence against the interests of the State and for the benefit of his client. However Becker claimed that the information that he had received was of little value in his defense of Sorro.[164]

By the time Becker's conduct was being exposed, he had turned over his defense of Sorro to the endlessly involved Walter Deuel. According to Assistant D.A. Pecora, this included sharing with Deuel "the entire case of the prosecution."[165]

Josephs Sorro and Cohen

Joseph Sorro's trial started on June 24, 1921. At least from a legal standpoint, one would finally find out whether his original testimony or his recantation was to be considered as the truth.

Governor Whitman's Former Deputy Attorney General, Alfred Becker, turned up as a defense witness for Sorro. He was questioned about turning over the confidential information about Sorro to Walter Deuel. However, Becker's testimony was that he had not done so.[166]

Philip Musica testified that his work as an investigator, in Governor Whitman's administration, made him the first to gather Sorro's information. At the time, according to Musica, Sorro reported hearing the plotters of Barnett's murder conferring about their plot. This meeting of Ippolito Greco, Jacob and Joseph Cohen, David Jacobs and Antonio Cardinale had occurred in Harlem.[167]

On July 14, 1921, Joseph Sorro was convicted of perjury. Legally, his original testimony was a lie, his recantation the truth. He would eventually be sentenced to ten to twenty years in prison.

Immediately upon Sorro's conviction, Cohen's Attorney, John J. Goldstein, announced that he would ask Governor Miller to pardon Joseph Cohen. Though Cohen might have plotted to murder Barnett, the State of New York had botched his prosecution. As revealed in Sorro's trial, Musica's "discovery" of Sorro's testimony [that was later judged to be perjury] was considered an unlawful conspiracy to convict Joseph Cohen.

Assistant District Attorney Pecora was aware that in prosecuting the perjury case he had compromised the conviction of Joseph Cohen. Like Senator Reed, he was and would continue to be an anti-corruption crusader. However, in the Baff Case, both Reed and Pecora pursued the letter of the law to the detriment of moral satisfaction.

Cohen did not receive an outright pardon, but the State did grant him a new trial, because his original conviction depended on Sorro's since discredited testimony. Bail was set at $20,000.[168] He was released from Sing Sing Prison, on November 23, 1921, pending his new trial. His release was expedited, at the request of his family, to enable him to join them for Thanksgiving Dinner.

Cohen left Sing Sing Prison protesting his innocence. He and his family were to have their holiday dinner at the home of his attorney on the seventh anniversary of Barnett's murder. The Baffs could have read that, in the New York Times, on Thanksgiving Day. It is unlikely that they were thankful. Over the years, Barnett's son Isadore/Irving would say, "I don't expect anything; that way I'm not disappointed."

What of Joseph Cohen's new trial? With scant evidence, besides Sorro's, and the departure, for Italy, of Cardinale, it seemed that the State could not effectively re-try Cohen. Cohen petitioned the court to dismiss his original indictment of January 1917. His petition presented him as innocent and wronged. He had been on death row; he had lost four years of his life; he had been stigmatized through perjured evidence. It would have been heart rending if it were all true, but someone who would order the murder of his business rival would have no trouble lying to a judge for his own freedom.

On February 6, 1922, a messenger was sent to Cohen's home to tell him: "The Court has just dismissed the indictment against you, and you will not be tried again on the charge of murdering Barnett Baff." Cohen was back in West Washington Market as a common laborer. He had lost the business for which he was willing to kill. His savings had been used up on lawyers. He was starting over, free and alive.[169]

By 1924, Cohen was back in the chicken pulling business and the chicken pullers association was taxing shippers an extra dollar for unloading live poultry from railroad cars. They were also limiting the number of chicken pullers leading to a high rate of pay. Additionally, they were claiming all chickens found dead and illegally selling them.[170]

So Far

In April 1922, the Grievance Committee of the New York State Bar Association did bring charges of professional misconduct against former Deputy Attorney General Alfred Becker in the Sorro perjury case. In reporting this latest development, the New York Times of April 22nd summarized legal outcomes to date:

> After eight years in the courts, the Baff case, which is said to be almost unique in its complicated after-history, has produced the following results:
>
> Former Deputy Attorney General Becker charged with unprofessional conduct.
>
> Walter Rogers Deuel, former Assistant District Attorney, indicted for subornation of perjury.
>
> Philip Musica, a former investigator on the staff of the Attorney General, indicted for subornation of perjury.
>
> Joseph Sorro, thrice-turned perjurer, sent to prison for ten years for perjury.
>
> Archiello [sic], who confessed to the actual murder of Baff, convicted and sent to the death house; granted a new trial at the request of the State on his claim of innocence; then again admits committing the murder and is allowed to plead guilty to manslaughter; gets suspended sentence.

> Joseph Cohen, the alleged "master mind" of
> the conspiracy, convicted and sent to the death
> house, chiefly on the testimony of Sorro;
> released by the Appellate Court after Sorro's
> conviction of perjury; charge against him
> dismissed when the State fails to apply for a
> new trial.

At this point, of the original Jewish conspirators and hired Sicilians, only two people remained in prison: Abraham Graff and Frank Ferrara. Neither was facing the death penalty. Even today when many oppose the death penalty, two men in Sing Sing is a skimpy result for a murder conspiracy of perhaps twenty-five poultrymen, two gunmen, a chauffeur, lookouts and go-betweens.

Going Forward

What the New York Times did not report, at this point, was that after being indicted for subornation of perjury, Philip Musica disappeared. He was to assume the name of a stranger, F. Donald Coster, and continue his life from there. By 1923, he had a new hair-related scheme. He started a hair tonic firm as the cover for a bootlegging operation.

In 1923, Alfred Smith returned to the New York State Governor's Mansion. Ferdinand Pecora, who had been so critical of Alfred Becker's professional conduct, was Acting District Attorney. Pecora pointed out that Graff's conviction had rested, in part, on Sorro's perjured testimony. He suggested that Governor Smith commute Graff's sentence. This lead to Graff being paroled about a year and five months early, after serving six years of his sentence.

In 1924, Barnett was in the news again, briefly. The City was burning the clothes that had been worn by murder victims. Barnett was mentioned along with Herman Rosenthal, as well as others.[171]

In 1928, just before completing his last term in office, Governor Smith commuted Frank Ferrara's sentence. This was done on the recommendation of the Judge before whom Ferrara was tried and with the concurrence of the District Attorney. Ferrara had been in prison for more than a dozen years. It is ironic that he served longer than any of the gunmen or murder conspirators. It was his arrest that had set all the other arrests in motion and created a good beginning to attempted law and order. As it turned out though, outcomes that could not be accomplished legally would be accomplished by the lives people lead.

Endings

In 1930, Gaetano Rina (or Reina), who was mentioned at one time as the second gunmen in the Baff case, was shot and killed. This occurred as he emerged from the apartment building, in the Bronx, where he kept his mistress. He kept his wife and nine children in an elaborate private house elsewhere in the Bronx. His wife disclaimed any knowledge of the other woman.

Though Rina was described as an ice dealer, his office had recently been the site of two murders. He had a loaded rifle and two boxes of cartridges in his car. His pockets disgorged a revolver and $804 (in Depression Era dollars).[172]

* * *

Barnett's widow, Fannie Baff, eventually supported herself by running a rooming house in Arverne, (Queens) New York. She died in 1931 having finally learned to read English under the tutelage of one of her granddaughters.

* * *

About a year later it was Joseph Cohen's turn. By this time, he had his own wholesale poultry business, Joseph Cohen and Brother, near West Washington Market. He was once again head of the chicken pullers "union." He owned 3 cars. He was living in a big house[173] in the pleasant Prospect Park South section of Brooklyn.

On the evening of April 8, 1932, Joseph Cohen was sitting on his enclosed porch, playing pinochle with his wife and his bodyguard. The door bell rang. Joseph Cohen opened the door and was shot nine times. Three gunman escaped in a waiting car. Unconscious, Cohen died soon after in Kings County Hospital without confessing to anything.

The police would investigate inconclusively whether this was part of a new plot among poultry dealers or an echo of the Baff case.[174] About a month later, Joseph Cohen's brother, Barney, a poultry and fish merchant, was shot multiple times from a car that sped away.

* * *

Harry Baff was also a crime victim, but not a murder victim. This was the case that, compared to Barnett's case, showed what might have been. By 1932, Harry and two partners had a business in West Washington Market. However, they were preyed upon by gangsters and decided to move to the Bronx. They set up at 2962 Park Avenue, in the Bronx, as S., S. & B. Live Poultry Corporation.

However, the gangsters did not need passports to come to the Bronx too. They wanted Harry and partners to pay protection in the form of renting crates and trucks from the criminal sources that they represented. They wanted to fix the wholesale price at which S., S. & B. Live Poultry Corporation bought its poultry. In other words, the gangsters wanted to make Harry et al. mere employees of their would-be kosher poultry monopoly. As Barnett had done in the days of the Poultry Trust, Harry and his partners starting buying directly from the farmers in the South and West.

The gangsters responded with theft of chickens, a stench bomb thrown into a store and breaking windows of S., S. & B.'s businesses. However, on the morning of April 6, 1933, they aroused the police's suspicions by circling twice around 2962 Park Avenue in a car and a taxi. The gangsters sneaked into the enclosure of the business under cover of an arriving truck. Not knowing that they were being observed by the police, the invaders began to smash everything in sight with oak billiard cues.[175] Then the arrests commenced.

The police had driven their car across the entrance to the business and called for help. The police had noticed suspicious behavior and acted on it. They had seven men under arrest. Samuel J. Foley, "the energetic new District Attorney in the Bronx"[176] wanted to prosecute. However Harry and his partners, Samuel Weiner (a.k.a.Werner), Samuel Shipper and Hyman Blank , were unwilling to be witnesses at the upcoming trial.

The D.A.'s office figured that Harry and partners were being intimidated. They sent Assistant D.A. William H. Jackson to court to have three partners and another witness held on bail of $25,000 each, as material witnesses.[177] The gangsters were not so readily foiled.

About 1:00 in the morning of April 23rd, a Sunday, Bronx D.A. Foley was served with a writ of habeas corpus for Harry Baff and the other three witnesses whom he had in custody, because someone had posted their bail of $25,000 per person. No one in the Bronx knew who had arranged bail and the writ. Further it was signed by Supreme Court Justice Mitchell May who asked the interested parties to appear in Room 1001 at the Hotel Commodore rather than in a courtroom. Again the Bronx authorities were suspicious and acted accordingly.

Harry and the other witnesses were heavily escorted by the police, the Bronx County Sheriff and D.A. Foley on their middle of the night trip to the Hotel. It was 2:00 a.m. by the time that they got to Room 1001. The room was crowded with relatives and friends of the witnesses. Justice May presided from behind a small desk.

The writ had been obtained by an attorney who said he was representing Samuel Werner's brother, Moe. It was later thought that Moe had been pressured to persuade Samuel to accept bail and leave the protection of jail. Moe said that Sam's wife was sick, Sam's business was falling apart without him and that he, Moe, was losing weight from stress. However, Samuel was hostile to his brother's intervention. D.A. Foley had to call the squabbling siblings to order.

Despite the unconventional situation, Justice May had the wit to ask each of the witnesses if he wanted to leave jail. No one did. The Judge dismissed the writ of habeas corpus and raised bail to $250,000 per "prisoner". The witnesses were hustled into a car with police cars fore and aft. They returned to jail with their protective custody intact. Not only would they be able to make the D.A.'s case against the criminal control of the poultry trade, but they were showing the strength of the law in thwarting gangsters in general. [178]

It was later discovered that the same man who bailed out one of the racketeers had been sent with the bail money for the poultry dealers. This served as another confirmation of the corrupt nature of the bail out attempt. The next day, Samuel Simberg, a night watchman at S., S. & B. Live Poultry Corporation, also requested protective custody. His bail was set at $300,000. The families of the witnesses also received police protection.

As it turned out, this latest attempt to control the live poultry trade was the work of one man,

Joseph Weiner, backed by a private squad of thugs. In effect, Weiner, aged 38, attempted to make all businesses in the kosher poultry industry work for his profit. He chose everyone's employees: freight handlers, chicken pluckers, ritual slaughterers. Trucks, crates and chicken feed were supplied through Weiner, too. He started his racket in other boroughs and attempted to extend it to the Bronx. His take was said to be $50,000 a week at a time when a working man made less than $100/week.

Joseph Weiner had also been questioned at the time of the shooting death of Joseph Cohen. He was operating under a restraining order against violating the Sherman Antitrust Act and he was guilty of violating that order. He had previously been indicted, but the indictment had been dismissed. The police would arrest him as soon as they found him.[179] Harry and his partners took out gun permits, bought 32 caliber pistols and did target practice.[180] Joseph Weiner was found, convicted and jailed. Samuel Foley was reelected District Attorney four times and elected to a Bronx County judgeship before his death in 1951.

* * *

Though the last echoes of the Baff case had not been heard, the roaring 20's had given way to the Great Depression. Assistant D.A. Ferdinand Pecora, who had questioned Deputy A.G. Becker so closely about his possible conflict of interest in the Sorro Case, had joined the Federal Government. He was chief counsel for the Senate Banking and Currency Committee in its investigation of the financial shenanigans that had lead to the stock market crash.

Pecora was brilliant and relentless; the securities industry investigation became known informally as the Pecora hearings. He laid the groundwork for the New Deal's regulation of the banks and brokerages and went on to become one of the commissioners of the Securities and Exchange Commission. One wonders what Pecora might have done with his good command of facts and his tenaciousness had he been the original prosecutor of the Baff case instead of the duplicitous Deuel. Just as Pecora embarrassed the wealthy in his later investigation, he might have embarrassed those who fought Barnett and the Baff's consumer friendly business model. He might have convicted the Jewish business men and gotten the conviction to stick.

* * *

Harry Baff passed away in 1937. His wife, Rose would live almost another 50 years and become a great-grandmother. William Baff died, childless, in 1969. Etta Baff Shaw was survived by two sons when she died in 1977. Isadore/Irving Baff died in 1985 with five grandchildren and since has acquired four great-grandchildren.

Philip Musica/F. Donald Coster

Just as the story of Harry Baff's business in the Bronx showed that the themes of rivalry and monopoly continued in the poultry industry, the theme of Musica's amoral greed continued too. To his hair tonic/bootlegging operation, in 1926, he added a drug firm, McKesson & Robbins. In 1928, he took the business public. After prohibition was repealed at the end of 1933, Musica, still under the cover of Coster, started bootlegging munitions. He shipped guns in cases labelled "milk of magnesia."[181] In 1938, he was readying a shipment to Spain though it is not known which side in their Civil War he was supplying.[182]

That same year, it was discovered that eighteen million dollars in assets were missing from McKesson & Robbins. Coster was arrested at the behest of the Securities and Exchange Commission. The most significant aspect was that he was fingerprinted and photographed. A former colleague of Musica's recognized Coster's picture and the police were able to match Musica's fingerprints to Coster's. First though they had to find Musica's fingerprints. One set had mysteriously disappeared from police headquarters. However another set was located at a neighborhood police station. It was also discovered that three of Musica's brothers were working at McKesson & Robbins under assumed names.

When Coster read in the morning paper that he had been unmasked as Musica, he guzzled some whiskey, locked himself in the bathroom, lay down in the bathtub and shot himself in the head. His life game of Russian Roulette concluded none too soon. Two U.S. marshals arrived within minutes of his death, but he had cheated the authorities one last time.

1938

Not only did 1938 see the passing of Musica, but it saw the murder of Barnett pass into the history of quirky murders. On May 22, 1938, *Murders Not Quite Solved*[183] received a brief review in the New York Times. Barnett's murder qualified, because of its complex aftermath.   Also, by emphasizing the subsequent murder of Ippolito Greco, the author, Alvin F. Harlow, introduces extra, though tangential, gore.

The New York Public Library still has this book in its research collection. Therefore it is possible to read it today.   It offers a description of West Washington Market and of the police work in Harlem's little Italy. There are sensational details of the murder of Ippolito Greco, the East Harlem saloon owner.   There is also some detail on Cardinale's flight to Italy.

Of course, West Washington Market still existed at the time that *Murders Not Quite Solved* was written*.   It also seems likely that author

---

* In 1941, the Queens Live Poultry Terminal opened. West Washington Market declined in importance and was demolished in 1950.

Harlow had an informant or two from the police department of an earlier era. This seems likely from the details he offers and from his praise for the police.

It seems however that Harlow does not always get the details right. There is an overemphasis on Barnett as a lone wolf. There is no background on who he was as a person or his history as an immigrant. He is referred to here, and (so far) no place else, as Barney. Harlow claims that all chicken pullers are gangsters. He probably gets the date wrong for the post murder pay-off in Greco's saloon. He definitely misstates the timing of Senator Reeds investigation. Though it is unconfirmed elsewhere, Harlow does offer some insight into Barnett's lack of police protection at the time of the murder. He says that Barnett called off his police guard, because he was annoyed by being followed.

By the time that *Murders Not Quite Solved* was published, Barnett's six grandchildren, born after his death, were old enough to read it. At least one of them did. About the time that some of their children were being born, *The New Yorker* published a profile of Philip Musica.[*] The author clearly subscribed to Musica's major role in derailing the Baff case.

Now it is the turn of Barnett's great-great grandchildren (the grandchildren's grandchildren) to read his story as a picture can be created from the pieces. If by clarifying the past, the present is more vivid, then the story has been worth telling. Besides, to quote Etta Baff, "There are still some of us left" and we are still reinventing ourselves in America.

Neither a kaleidoscope, nor a great-grandfather, is entirely lost as long as it lingers in memory.

---

[*] Robert Shaplan, Annals of Crime, "The Metamorphosis of Philip Musica", October 22, 1955. I remember my mother, a *New Yorker* subscriber, reading it and marveling over the disappearance of files involving Barnett's murder.

Appendix A: Field Trip to 31 Henry Street

The City Directory of 1891-1892 lists Barnett as a grocer at 31 Henry Street. My son, Isaac, helped me find 31 Henry Street in Google Earth. It appeared to be an older building and therefore worth a look. I thought perhaps it was an actual building in which Barnett worked and lived.

We took the Q train to the Canal Street subway station. Though there were trains and elevated trains in 1892, the first true subway did not open until 1904. The only above ground part of our route went over the Manhattan Bridge which wasn't built until the first decade of the 20th century. In 1891 the only bridge between New York (Manhattan) and Brooklyn was the Brooklyn Bridge. However, there was ferry service on the East River.

The walk from Canal and Centre Streets to 31 Henry Street took us through part of Chinatown. Most of the buildings were old, but not necessarily as old as 1892. It was hard to tell about 31 Henry. It is currently a red brick building with green trim, probably painted cast iron, and some stone trim above the windows. It's five stories tall with the large windows of a commercial space on the ground floor.

The building at 35 Henry Street is probably too recent for Barnett's tenure on the block. It was built in 1897. There are two very dilapidated old buildings on the block that have the simple style and small size of the early nineteenth century. They are under renovation and would have been in better shape when Barnett, Fannie and Harry passed by them. William Baff may have been born at 31 Henry Street.

A block and a half south, on Oliver Street, there are Federalist Era brick buildings in better shape. They might have been seen by George Washington, when New York City was capital of the United States, and definitely by Barnett. There is also a Greek Revival Baptist Church that needs restoring.

This is a neighborhood that has been seeing immigrants arrive in this country since the Dutch showed up. Now it is the province of the Chinese with a few Vietnamese restaurants around the edges. The buildings wear out, get renovated or replaced. The people move on to the newer neighborhoods or the suburbs. There is still some sense of the enduring process of which Barnett was a part and, if the streets could talk, I would stand there for hours taking notes. However, since they can't, I went on line and found out that construction of the current 31 Henry Street wasn't completed until 1910. Barnett probably lived in an old building that had been contemporaneous with George Washington, two founding fathers with the streets of New York in common.

Appendix B: On The Trail of West Washington Market

West Washington Market was built out into the Hudson River in what is today the Meat Packing District. The streets of this part of town, adjacent to Greenwich Village, are unmoored from the rest of Manhattan's grid. They are the evidence of a seventeenth century settlement separate from New Amsterdam/New York.

By the late nineteenth century, the area near the Hudson River was industrial. Presumably the availability of boat transportation encouraged this development. In fact, in December 1888, when the new West Washington Market was opened, new docks were going to be built on the site of the old Market.[184]

Ferry service was the only direct connection between Manhattan and New Jersey until the 1930's. Though completed in 1825, the Erie Canal, which connected the Hudson River to the Midwest, was still being enlarged at the time of Barnett's murder.

The new West Washington Market had streets named Lawton, Loew, Hewitt, Tompkins and Grace Avenues. These streets, which no longer exist, make it harder to comprehend the description of Barnett's murder.

The best way to get to the site is to walk west on 13th Street until it butts into Horatio Street and continue west on Horatio. At the junction is Jackson Square with a small, triangular park surrounding a tall fountain. Along the six block walk west, there is lower scale housing of mixed historical periods. There are simple, early 19th century, brick townhouses, tenements and one taller 1920's era apartment building. Closer to the river, there are old commercial buildings, probably converted to residential lofts since the 1970's.

At Washington Street, the first connection to the old commercial nature of the Hudson shore is a glimpse of the High Line. This is what remains of an old freight line, above the street, on a parallel with the third story of old commercial buildings. Astride the High Line, there is a huge glass and steel building. The old railway, itself, has been recycled as a park. However, the High Line wasn't built until the late 1920's. In Barnett's day, there were much more dangerous street level tracks serving the West Side of Manhattan.

One block further, at West Street, is a white on green road sign: Meat Market, Exit 4. Across the street is the newly developed Hudson River Park. It is cleverly landscaped to inject variety into a narrow strip of land that occasionally bumps out onto a pier. It takes the shore back from industry and back from Robert Moses's girdle of highways and gives it to New Yorkers for recreation.

About one block north is the entrance to the City's Department of Sanitation site that replaced the New West Washington Market of Barnett's day. It appears to be about two square blocks built out into the river. The land-front is a swath of rose bushes, the interior undistinguished buildings and a parking lot full of garbage trucks. It is a spot from which ocean liners, barges, tugboats, ferries and sail boats are, and were, visible. Small waves break around its rocky edges and the wind is fierce in winter; sun reflects hot from the water in summer. There is a slight brackish whiff to the air. Here, at its southern end, the Hudson River is a tidal estuary.

Across the traffic of West Street, facing the rose bushes, are The Gansevoort Market – West Center, Interstate Foods and Premier Veal. Here is a little evidence of the old meat market days along this one block. To the south are fancy new residences with river views.

A little more of my curiosity about Barnett is satisfied. The elements of extreme weather, tide, rail and river traffic are still in evidence. This place, built on battered rocks, is about ignoring difficulties and accomplishing one's business. Under the newly planted bed of roses a ruthless environment lingers.

Appendix C: Irving Gets Arrested in Central Park

As told by Irving Baff to the three oldest of his four granddaughters on June 23, 1979.

Transcribed and Edited by Bonnie Quint Kaplan.

When I was about 16 years old, I had a friend named Harry Rosen. We used to pal together and on a Saturday we decided to hire a rowboat in Central Park and go rowing. While we were out rowing, it was about time to come in, because we had hired the boat for an hour, (or perhaps two hours, whatever it was). As we neared shore, we noticed that a policeman caught a little boy who was fishing. So I yelled out, "let him go." My friend, Harry yelled, "let him go, you big stiff."

So, as we went to get ashore, the policeman came over toward us and as he did, we rowed back onto the lake again. We stayed out another half hour and we tried it again. The cop still met us over there, so we went out a third time. And the third time, when we came back, we didn't see the cop. So we got ashore, but the cop fooled us, because he was in the boathouse, hiding. When we came in, he arrested us. That was on a Saturday morning at about 10:00 or 11:00 o'clock and they took us down to the police arsenal at 65th Street and Fifth Avenue and they held us for Night Court.

When we went to Night Court, which was about 8:00 o'clock in the evening or perhaps a little later, we went before the judge and the judge asked what the charge was. And [there was] this big cop and we little sixteen year olds looked so insignificant [compared] to him. He said, "they called me a big stiff."

So the judge even smiled and the judge said, "I fine you two dollars, each." He hesitated on the "each." And luckily, I had the money and my friend didn't have any money. So I paid the money and we were released.

When we came out, I saw the headline in the paper. There was [sic] two fighters that fought that day, which was a very important heavy weight bout between, I think, it was Luther McCarthy and Arthur Pelkey. One of them was knocked out and died in the ring. By that, you can always find out what day it was*.

---

* It took me 30 years and the story of Barnett, but I finally researched the date of the fight. It was May 14, 1913 and Arthur Pelkey ko'd Luther McCarthy, in Calgary, Alberta.

Notes

---

[1] Based on his gravestone, in Brooklyn's Washington Cemetery. Based on Irving Baff's birth certificate and census data, Barnett may have been born as early as 1857. Based on his death certificate, he was born in 1863.

[2] Based on her gravestone, in Brooklyn's Washington Cemetery. This is consistent with Irving's birth certificate. However, based on census data, she was born in 1865.

[3] This is consistent with Harry's death certificate and census data.

[4] Based on two separate census's (1910 and 1920).

[5] Based on Irving's birth certificate.

[6] This is confirmed by Samuel Baff's World War II Draft Registration Card.

[7] However we know from listings for wife, Frances, that he kept his hand in groceries for a while. The 1894-1895 directory has Frances as a grocer at 864 First Avenue (approximately 49th Street). The 1895-1896 directory lists her with a grocery at 1190 Third Avenue (approximately 70th Street) and a residence at 965 First Avenue (approximately 57th Street).

[8] Rischin, Moses, *The Promised City, New York's Jews, 1870-1914.*

[9] 1901-1902 City Directory

[10] The city directories of 1903-1904 through 1905-1906, show two new business locations for the Baffs, nothing new residential. Barnett had a meat business at 62 East 110th Street and a poultry business (with Harry and Samuel Baff) at 618 West 39th Street. The 1906-1907 directory replaces the 62 East 110th Street address with a poultry business at 526 East 80th Street which still existed when Barnett's estate was settled in 1916. The 1906-1907 directory also picks up the trail of residences at 16 East 110th Street, in East Harlem, then a Jewish neighborhood. After that the West 39th Street location is no longer listed and Barnett lives at 1652 Madison Avenue (approximately 111th Street), then 22 East 109th Street. Finally in 1913, Barnett is listed at his ultimate address 76 West 120th Street, Harlem.

[11] Jeffrey S Gurock, *When Harlem Was Jewish, 1870-1930*

[12] NY Times 12/23/1914

[13] NY Times 12/23, 27/1914

[14] NY Tribune, 11/25/1914

[15] NY Times 12/14/1906

[16] New York Times, August 4, 1911

17 http://www.encyclopedia.com/topic/William_Travers_Jerome.aspx

[18] NY Times, June 20, 1911

[19] NY Times, 7/8/1911

[20] NY Times, 8/ 8/1911

[21] NY Times, 5/12/1936

[22] NY Times, 8/17/1911

[23] NY Times, 8/26/1911

[24] NY Times, 2/7/1914

[25] New York Times, November 28, 1914

[26] Irving Howe, *World of Our Fathers,* p. 117

[27] Irving Howe, *World of Our Fathers,* p. 164.

[28] New York Times 12/3/1914

[29] NY Times 11/18/1914

[30] NY Herald Tribune, 7/3/1932

[31] NY Times, 12/17/1914

[32] NY Tribune, 7/13/1913

[33] NY Tribune, 6/27/1917

[34] NY Times 6/30/1917

[35] NY Tribune, 7/13/1913

[36] NY Times 6/30/17

[37] NY Times 6/30/17

[38] NY Tribune, 11/28/1916

[39] NY Times 4/6/16

[40] NY Times 11/26/1914

[41] Pawtucket (RI) Times, November 27,1914

[42] NY Times 2/13/16

[43] NY Times 12/25/1914

[44] NY Times 6/27/1917

[45] NY Times 6/27/1917

[46] NY Times 6/28/1917

[47] NY Times 5/15/1915

[48] NY Times 11/28/1914

[49] NY Times 2/13/1916

[50] NY Times 2/13/1916

[51] NY Times 11/25/1914

[52] NY Times 11/26/1914

[53] NY Times 2/10/1916, 4/22/22, 4/6/1916

[54] NY Times 2/12/1916

[55] New York Times 6/28/1917, 12/5/1914

[56] NY Times 7/11/1917

[57] NY Times 2/16/1916

[58] Washington Post, 11/26/1914

[59] NY Times 6/28/1917,12/3/1914, 2/12/1916

[60] NY Times 12/29/1914

[61] NY Times 7/17/1917, 11/26/1914
[62] NY Times 2/11/1916, 12/1/1914
[63] NY Times 11/26/1914
[64] NY Times 7/11/17, 11/25/1914
[65] NY Times 11/28/1914
[66] NY Times 12/3/1914
[67] NY Times 12/3/1914, 6/27/1917, 7/11/1917
[68] NYTribune, 11/25/14
[69] NY Times 12/1/1914, 12/3/1914, 2/10/1916
[70] NY Tribune, 12/1/1914
[71] NY Times 7/11/17, 6/28/1917, 12/5/14
[72] NY Times 11/25/1914
[73] NY Times 2/10/1916, 2/11/1916
[74] NY Times 6/28/1917
[75] NY Times 11/27/1914
[76] New York Times 12/3/1914
[77] Richmond Times-Dispatch, 2/27/1916
[78] Philadelphia Inquirer 12/21/1914
[79] New York Times 12/20/1914
[80] NY Times 12/23/1914, 12/3/1914
[81] NY Times 12/21/1914
[82] Boston Herald 11/30/1914
[83] New York Times 12/05/1914
[84] NY Times 12/23/1914, 12/1/1914, 12/5/1914
[85] New York Times 12/31/1914
[86] 1/2/1915
[87] Idaho Statesman, 12/2/1914
[88] Quoted in The State, of Columbia, SC, 12/4/1914
[89] Springfield (MA) Union, 2/1/1915
[90] New York Times 6/15/1915
[91] New York Times 6/16/1915
[92] *Against the Evidence,* New York: 1970, The McCall Publishing Company
[93] NY Times 12/3/1914
[94] NY Times 2/10/1916
[95] NY Times 2/13/1916, 2/11/1916
[96] NY Times 2/12/1916, 2/14/1916, 2/15/1916
[97] NY Times 2/14/1916
[98] NY Times 2/13/1916
[99] NY Times 2/14/1916
[100] NY Times 2/16/1916, 2/17/1916, 3/28/1916
[101] NY Times 2/17/1917
[102] NY Times 4/6/1916
[103] NY Times 4/7/1916

[104] NY Times 4/8/1916
[105] NY Times 4/8/1916
[106] NY Times 4/10/1916
[107] NY Times 4/12/1916
[108] NY Times 4/13/1916
[109] NY Times 4/14/1916
[110] New York Times 5/16/1916
[111] NY Times 4/4/1919
[112] NY Times 1/16/1917
[113] NY Times 1/13/1917
[114] NY Times 3/23/1917
[115] New York Times 3/31/1917
[116] NY Times 4/7/1917
[117] New York Times 4/22/1922
[118] NY Times 10/16/1919
[119] NY Times 5/26/1917
[120] New York Times 5/27/1917
[121] NY Times 6/15/1917
[122] NY Times 6/26/1917
[123] NY Times 6/27/1917
[124] NY Times 6/27/1917
[125] NY Times 6/28/1917
[126] Boston Herald, 6/29/1917
[127] NY Times 6/30/1917
[128] NY Times 7/3/1917
[129] NY Times 7/6/1917
[130] NY Times 7/6/1917
[131] NY Times 7/7/1917
[132] NY Times 7/7/1917
[133] NY Times 7/11/1917, 7/17/1917
[134] NY Times 7/20/1917
[135] NY Times 7/21/1917
[136] NY Times 8/18/1917
[137] NY Times 8/18/1917
[138] NY Times 8/4/1917
[139] NY Times 2/13/1918
[140] NY Times 7/17/1918
[141] NY Times 7/2/1918
[142] NY Times 12/3/1918
[143] NY Times 12/12/1918
[144] NY Times 1/11/1919
[145] NY Times 1/11/1919
[146] NY Tribune, 3/12/1919
[147] NY Times 3/8/1919

[148] NY Times 4/3/1919
[149] NY Times 6/7/1919
[150] NY Times 8/25/1919, 10/16/1919
[151] NY Times 3/20/1926
[152] NY Times 10/16/1919
[153] NY Times 12/6/1919
[154] NY Times 12/7/1919
[155] NY Times 11/20/1919
[156] NY Times 2/6/1920, 12/11/1919
[157] NY Times 2/8/1920
[158] *Hey Rub-a-Dub-Dub,* page 45
[159] NY Times 2/21/1920
[160] NY Times 4/27/1920
[161] NY Times 4/28/1920
[162] NY Times 1/11/1921
[163] NY Times 3/24/1921
[164] NY Times 4/19/1921
[165] NY Times 7/9/1921
[166] NY Times 7/12/1921
[167] NY Times 7/9/1921
[168] NY Times 12/15/1921
[169] NY Times 2/7/1922
[170] NY Herald Tribune, 8/21/1924, 8/22/1924
[171] NY Tribune, 6/29/1924
[172] NY Times 2/27/1930
[173] NY Herald Tribune 4/9/1932
[174] NY Times 4/9/1932
[175] NY Times 4/7/1933
[176] NY Herald Tribune, 4/25/1933
[177] NY Times 4/21/1933
[178] NY Times 4/23/1933, 4/24/1933
[179] NY Times 4/24/1933, 4/25/33
[180] NY Herald Tribune, 5/14/1933
[181] Washington Post, 12/16/1938
[182] Washington Post, 12/22/1938
[183] By Alvin F. Harlow, New York: Julian Messner, Inc.
[184] NY Times 11/10/1888

Made in the USA
Middletown, DE
24 October 2015